THE *Speaker's* VOICE

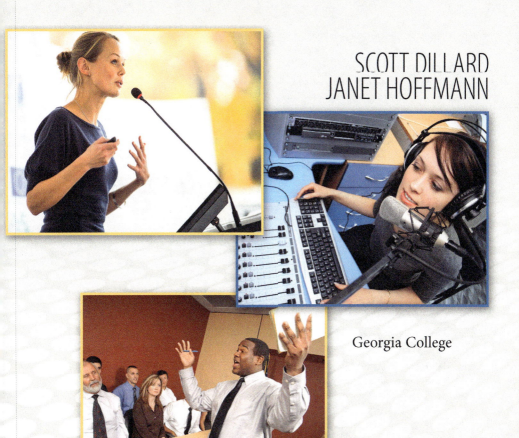

SCOTT DILLARD
JANET HOFFMANN

Georgia College

Kendall Hunt
publishing company

Cover image © Shutterstock, Inc.

www.kendallhunt.com
Send all inquiries to:
4050 Westmark Drive
Dubuque, IA 52004-1840

It took me quite a long time to develop a voice, and now that I have it, I am not going to be silent.

—Madeleine Albright

Contents

"Words mean more than what is set down on paper. It takes the human voice to infuse them with deeper meaning."

—Maya Angelou

Why We Wrote This Book

Many of us began our formal study of communication by taking a course in basic public speaking. One feature of most public speaking textbooks is a single chapter devoted to vocal delivery and/or the use of the voice in effective oratory.

Rarely can an instructor of basic public speaking devote more than a day or two of sustained work on maximizing the power of students' voices as a vital component of speaking excellence. A quick glance at evaluation sheets for public speaking, however, will show that much of what is evaluated and how well students express themselves is through their voice. We contend then that a more sustained emphasis needs to be placed on developing the voice of the speaker. Many programs in communication lack a stand-alone voice and diction course. We created this companion handbook as a way to close that gap.

Students who plan to go into careers in teaching, ministry, law, podcasting, broadcasting, and performing arts need sustained attention to their vocal production. It is for these students that we wrote this book.

Teachers who work in the fields of communication or theatre should find this text to be a valuable resource for a course in voice or as a supplemental resource in other courses such as public speaking, oral interpretation, performance studies, acting, or broadcasting. Using this text alongside traditional texts in those courses will allow the teacher to provide additional individualized attention to students vocal development.

The Legacy/Value/History of Voice Training for Speakers

This book you are reading, *The Speaker's Voice* as well as any other current textbook designed to enhance the oral communication skills and abilities of citizens living in democratic societies can trace its lineage back almost 2,500 years, to the island of Sicily, in the city of Syracuse, around 467 BC. Land disputes at that time were typically settled by violent means as there were no lawyers to plead for the legitimacy of one litigant's claims over another's. An enterprising rhetorician by the name of Corax wrote down a five-part organizational pattern and argument advice designed to maximize the persuasive power of the citizen-speaker's claims (Ryan 5–6). The text was called "Techne" for "technique," and it began a four-hundred-year trajectory of theoretical and practical advancement in oral persuasion still studied and practiced by those who want to make their mark or their living using the power of their voice to influence others.

It is way beyond our ability to try to summarize the plethora of contributions of the Greek and Roman rhetorical teachers and theorists to our current knowledge of best practices in vocal delivery for speakers. We urge you to explore the origins of rhetoric and oratory by reading such texts as Kennedy's work. In the next few pages, we want to pay homage to several of the most influential early Greek and Roman teachers and practitioners of the art and craft of vocal delivery.

The sixth and fifth centuries of BC in Greece marked the transformation of rule by aristocracy to rule by democracy. As Herrick notes, Corax's "systematic approach to teaching oratory was quickly adapted by others, and was carried to Athens and other Greek city-states by professional teachers and practitioners of rhetoric known as Sophists" (32). The bourgeoning market for their services had a lot to do with the fact that in Athenian trials citizens delivered their own speeches of prosecution and defense to a jury of several hundred randomly chosen citizens. As Herrick notes "Beginning around 430 B.C. speech writers or logographers like the sophist Antiphon could be hired to write a courtroom speech. Interpretation of what laws there were was less significant than was the individual citizen's persuasive speech before a large audience. Immediately following the two speeches a vote was taken and the majority prevailed. Thus skill in speaking was paramount in Athenian courts, for the most persuasive public speaker carried the day" (34).

One of the best-known speechwriters and orators was Demosthenes (384–322 BC). As recounted by Ryan, "When asked what were the three most important functions in persuasive speaking, Demosthenes is reported to have said 'delivery, delivery, delivery'" (81). Ryan also notes that "Demosthenes was a student of Isocrates and overcame through hard work (as his teacher said one could) two distinct disadvantages: Demosthenes stammered, so he practiced with a pebble in his mouth to force correct articulation and had a naturally weak voice, so he went to the sea shore and recited poetry over the sound of the waves" (Ryan 11).

Another well-known Sophist or "wise teacher" was Hippias of Elis, the father of mnemonics or memory training. Sophists taught their students to deliver all their speeches from memory, and Hippias developed numerous techniques for accurately recalling a prepared text in the process of orally delivering it. Most well known and still advocated today is the technique of mentally visualizing a house, then as you are practicing and memorizing, place each part of your prepared text in a particular room. For example, place your introduction in the foyer, your first point in the kitchen, your second point in the dining room, your third point in the living room, and your conclusion on the back porch. Having secured those message-place associations, when you deliver your message all you have to do to trigger the accurate next words is to walk yourself through the house. Voila!

A contemporary of Hippias was Thrasymachus of Chalcedonia. "He advised his students to employ rhythm or vocal pacing in the voice to affect persuasion. He also taught his students to vary their pitches and inflections and to couple them with gestures to tap the audience's emotions" (Ryan 7).

One of the most influential teachers and practitioners of rhetorical virtuosity was Gorgias of Leontini, Sicily. He is purported to have lived from 485–380 BC, making him 105 years old when he expired. Famous for his defense of (encomium to) Helen of Troy, he exploited the magical, hypnotic power of words to seduce an audience and popularized rhetorical devices that created rhythm, momentum, and balance such as anaphora, epistrophe, and antithesis. He believed that the "sounds of words when manipulated with skill, could captivate audiences" (Herrick 42).

The two Roman rhetorical teachers and model practitioners whose works still influence us today are Cicero and Quintilian. Marcus Tullius Cicero (106–43 BC) was a lawyer, a member of the Roman Senate, and an eyewitness to the assassination of Julius Ceasar on the ides of March in 44 BC. The most eloquent and powerful of advocates for a democratic government, he was assassinated because of his success by a triumvirate of would-be dictators, and his head and hands were nailed to the speaker's podium in the Roman forum as a lesson to others who dared to advocate for democratic self-rule. Cicero introduced the five canons of rhetoric which constituted the key categories of skills a speaker must develop; invention, organization, language/style, delivery, and memory. While memory referred to the previously mentioned skills regarding memorizing a prepared message, he separated out vocal delivery (pronuntiatio in Latin) as "the control of voice and body in a manner suitable to the dignity of the subject matter and the style. A speech in a Roman courtroom or in the Senate was a performance, and the skilled orator needed the presence, poise, power, and grace of an actor. Orators studied movement, gestures, posture, facial expression, and vocal tone and volume" (Herrick 98).

The greatest Roman teacher of the art of eloquent and persuasive speaking is generally acknowledged to be Marcus Fabius Quintilianus (35–100 AD), better known as Quintilian. His treatise *The Institutes of Oratory* is a complete guide to public speaking. He is most often cited for his definition of the art of rhetoric as consisting of a good citizen speaking well. He incorporated all of the theory and practical delivery advice of the Greek and Roman Speech teachers and scholars who preceded him, and added more detailed advice about voice and gesture. "Quintilian noted that Romans dreaded monotones, disliked singsong speakers, did not appreciate being sprayed with the speaker's saliva, objected to speakers that inhaled loudly, and complained about overly nasal voices. He was also annoyed with speakers who sawed the air with their hands, rubbed their noses, walked up and down when delivering the speech, and shifted their weight from foot to foot" (Ryan 82).

The Greek and Roman teachers of voice thought its highest and most important use was for the improvement of the human condition and in the service of democratic self-government. Their work laid a solid foundation for later theory and practice.

Skipping forward from the ancient rhetoricians of Greece and Rome, the elocutionary movement would be the next great flowering of concern for instruction of the voice for oratory.

The elocutionary movement emerged as a formal discipline in the eighteenth century first in England and then later in America. Thomas Sheridan's work *Lectures on Elocution* and *Lectures on Reading* provided the student of oratory and public performance a series of directions for marking a text and reading aloud literary selections.

The rise in the nineteenth century of a middle class in America created a desire for self-improvement and betterment. The Lyceum movement arose as an answer for providing the masses with educational and entertainment programming. Lyceum programs would feature oratory by politicians and preachers, debates, readings, and instructional programs.

The Lyceum movement was primarily an urban phenomenon. The Chatauqua movement however was not only in the urban centers but also small towns throughout the Northeast and Midwest. The Chautauquas were multiple day events that would bring the surrounding communities together for those few days to hear the speakers, readers, and debates of the day.

These movements would require and create an interest for the improvement of oral presentation skills. Private schools of elocution began to open as a way to train professional speakers and to educate the young man or woman on proper diction and speaking. It would be a significant way to mark your education level and perhaps upward class mobility to have a learned speaking voice.

Eventually, the teaching of elocution would enter into public school systems and higher education. Young students would read from popular readers of the day like *McGuffey's New Juvenile Speaker*. Students in higher education would learn the art of declamation of famous speeches and passages from classical literature.

The elocutionary movement had two schools of thought about best practices for the training of the voice. The mechanical and the natural school were two ways of approaching the art form. Those more aligned with the mechanical school sought to codify the ways in which a person should speak prescribing what the voice and the body should do in order to express a particular emotion or attitude. Texts in this school would often include diagrams showing proper body positions for various emotions.

The natural school believed that no such prescriptions were needed but that, rather, the speaker need to only connect to the emotions and feel them to ensure a naturalistic and effective performance.

Most practitioners would pull from both schools in practice. However, some of the excesses of the more mechanical school began to give elocution a bad name as the performances they created fell out of favor with the public.

This falling out of favor for elocution didn't mean the end of vocal training. What elocutionists often did was shift the name of their field of study from elocution to expression. This is what S.S. Curry did. Curry, along with his wife Anna Baright would open a private school of elocution in Boston which would later become Curry College which still exists. Curry began calling what he did "expression" and wrote a good number of books in the field.

The following is a quote of Curry's speaking to the essential need for vocal training to create a clear, dynamic, controlled voice that would be able to clearly express a variety of feelings.

> The statement that if a man has the thought
> and is stirred by the feeling he will be likely to
> say it right, is true, if the man were normal, if
> all the channels of expression were open and if
> the man were free from bad habits. But to give
> no attention to habit or right or wrong modes
> of execution, to have no regard for unbalanced
> emotional conditions or perverted channels of
> expression, is to abandon men to all sorts of
> wild impulses and to reduce all oratorical
> delivery to chaos. (Curry 333–334)

As departments of speech communication arose, voice classes were often a part of the curriculum. The delivery skills needed in public address and in the oral interpretation of literature were essential to the enterprise. However, as the field of communication began to develop more specializations such as the study of interpersonal communication, small group communication, and organizational communication, the course in voice started to seem less essential and the voice course started to disappear from many curriculums.

This book is designed to be a corrective to the disappearance of voice training in the communication curriculum. Good delivery skills are still needed to succeed as speakers and attention should still be paid to developing a clear, strong vocal presence.

Our Philosophy of Promoting Your Native Eloquence, Your Authentic Voice

> When I first started out, being from the South and going to New York or Chicago, people kept telling me to get voice lessons and 'lose that stupid accent you got.' And I'm like, 'Well, where I come from, you have the stupid accent.'
>
> —JEFF FOXWORTHY

In working with the voice it is important for us to say what we are offering in this text and what we are not. We are interested in helping speakers use your own unique vocal qualities in a lively and perhaps, more flexible manner, expanding your expressive range, and responding to a variety of speaking contexts. We believe in isolating and closely examining each element of vocal expression such as volume, rate, pitch, pausing, and phrasing in order expand your vocal repertoire.

We take as our starting point the notion of **Native Eloquence** expressed by Rodenburg, who explains this concept in this way,

> I believe that all of us can speak with the native eloquence of poets and frequently do when the powerful need arises. Once we commit ourselves to simply knowing and needing a word, a good part of the speaking task is already accomplished. Speaking, in my mind, is not and never should be about refining accents or forcing our voice or speech into artificial moulds. It is about gaining a passionate commitment to words through a well-primed, free voice. It is letting our own eloquence speak for itself (14).

Rodenburg is interested in letting each of our voices shine in its own unique manner. It is not about, and we believe this as well, shaping your voice into some preconceived manner of speech that must conform to conventions that are not in keeping with your unique needs and style. She states that, "Rhetoric when linked with an individual's inner truth and need become a potent force" (14). It is this potent, individualistic force that we seek to awaken in this book.

There is not, in this book, a desire to make students conform to a standard accent or dialect of speech. We believe that the sound of an individual's voice is part of their identity and as such is a necessary part of their power as a speaker and a person in the world. An accent is simply a manner of speaking that derives from the speaker's native language and the environment in which speakers acquired language. We often attach meaning to the accents that we hear and as such we tend to perhaps, have a kind of snobbery about what a preferred accent might be. The media often reinforces this type of snobbery by focusing on certain accents as the preferred accents for newscasters or in print as a manner of showing a "correct" manner of speech. However, no accent or dialect is inherently better than another.

To illustrate the artificiality of a preferred dialect let us look at a preferred accent dialect from the past that is no longer much in use and now sounds artificial to our contemporary ears. If you listen to old broadcasts or watch movies from the nineteen thirties or forties you will hear an accent that today has no analog in our present-day media. This accent, the Transatlantic accent, is a purely artificial accent. It was adopted by those in the media to adhere to the technology of the times. It was a manner of speaking that was adopted and taught in elite schools in the Northeast of the United States and is a mix of American and British accents that favors neither. It became the way that broadcasters and actors of the time spoke. Texts such as **Speak with Distinction** by Edith Skinner helped popularize this manner of speech for the upper class, actors, and broadcasters.

So, although our emphasis in this book is not on accent reduction or elimination, it should be noted that there is still a preferred dialect of speech accent in much of the media and that is the Standard American Dialect. This dialect according to Glenn, Glenn, and Foreman

"is associated most often with educated Americans, with Caucasian descendants of settlers from England, and with people living in parts of the North, Midwest, and West. There is a common misconception that speakers of Standard American have *no* dialect, that only people from places such as Alabama or New Jersey talk in a marked way. This is wrong – every person speaks with a dialect, choosing ways to pronounce sounds. Standard American is one dialect, and in this country it is the dialect most commonly accepted and employed in the entertainment, education, business, and political worlds." (9)

So, although we are not interested in students acquiring a Standard American Dialect, we are aware that such a dialect is often preferred. As such we know that there may be a compelling need for some students to study and acquire such a dialect to move forward within their careers. We believe, however, that students should not eliminate their native accents and native eloquence but rather should employ a process of code shifting. Code Shifting is the process of using a particular standard for some audiences and shifting to another code for others. So, a person with a strong Southern accent for instance, should not totally eliminate their Southern accent but rather employ it strategically and learn to switch from their strong Southern accent when speaking to audiences with a preference for a different accent.

Whereas Glenn, Glenn, and Forman, in their text ask that you gain proficiency in Standard American English without losing the way you have always spoken (in essence arguing for code switching) we take an approach much closer to Wells who when describing what a good voice is says

> A good voice is clear and strong. It should be well supported by adequate breath control so that it projects well. A good voice is one that communicates messages at an appropriate rate, at a pitch level that is appropriate to the speaker and message. A good voice should be resonant and varied, articulating each sound clearly in connected speech. As a result of these qualities, a good voice makes a positive impression. In using such a voice, you will have altered for the better your self-image as you see people reacting more positively toward you (13).

Many textbooks in voice focus their attention on the acquisition of the International Phonetic Alphabet (IPA). Textbooks that are written within the field of communication studies have particularly taken this approach. The IPA is a universal alphabet of symbols that correspond to phonemes or basic units of sound or a sound family. Within the IPA there are forty-three phonemes (twenty-five are consonants and eighteen are vowels). In learning the phonetic alphabet, you can write phonetically in any language. Learning this system helps one attend to the variety of sounds that speech actually produces.

What the study of IPA may lack, however, is any real concentration on creating lively expressive voices. Simply learning sounds does not guarantee that one will be able to express those sounds with any true meaning or conviction with any Native Eloquence. So, the IPA is not emphasized in this book but is mentioned for those who wish to learn this system to remember or acquire correct pronunciation of words.

In short, we are advocating that students attend to the various aspects of vocal production such as volume, rate, pitch, pause, and phrasing to communicate clearly what they intend. We are hoping that by drilling in each of these areas, students of voice will create a greater range of expression and will have at their disposal a greater flexibility with their voices.

2

"Speech is the voice of the heart."

—ANNA QUINDLEN

The Need to Breathe: The Mechanics of Breathing and Speaking

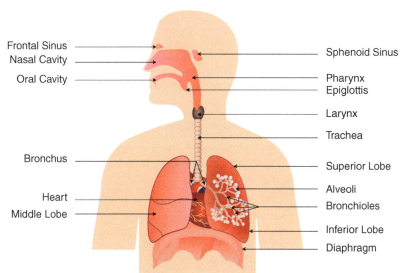

Frontal Sinus
Nasal Cavity
Oral Cavity
Bronchus
Heart
Middle Lobe

Sphenoid Sinus
Pharynx
Epiglottis
Larynx
Trachea
Superior Lobe
Alveoli
Bronchioles
Inferior Lobe
Diaphragm

©stockshoppe/Shutterstock.com

The parts of our anatomy that are used to speak are also used for other purposes. Speaking is a secondary biological function as all of the basic anatomical parts used in speech are also used for other purposes. Much of the anatomy that is used in speech is also used in ordinary breathing and as such, speech and breathing and breath control in speaking are intimately linked.

The parts of our body that are used to speak can be broken down in to three areas: (1) Phonation, which includes the larynx, vocal folds, glottis, and epiglottis, (2) Resonation, which includes the use of the pharynx, oral cavity, and the nasal cavity, and (3) Articulation, which includes the lips, tongue, hard and soft palate, lower jaw, and the gums.

Phonation is the process of vibrating the vocal chords for initial production of speech. Resonation is the amplification and modification of the sound originated in the larynx. Articulation is the production of the individual sounds or phonemes of a given language.

When we breathe we take air into our lungs through the process of respiration or inhalation and exhalation. Contracting and relaxing the diaphragm controls this process of respiration. The diaphragm is a muscle located under the lungs and when it contracts air is taken in to the lungs allowing them to expand. When breathing normally you can see the expansion of the stomach pushing outward when the diaphragm expands and on an exhalation the stomach moving inward as air is pushed back out of the lungs.

Becoming aware of the breath is one of the first steps you can take in becoming more aware of the mechanics of speech. If you put your hand on the top part of your abdomen below the rib cage and breathe you will see your hand rise and fall in concert with the inhalation and exhalation of the breathe. Taking a breath in and holding it and then slowly exhaling will indicate the control of breathe that you have and ultimately the amount of breath you can use in a given unit of speech.

The trachea is commonly called the windpipe. It allows the passage of air to flow from the lungs into the larynx. Once air is expelled from the lungs through the trachea it arrives at the larynx where the vocal folds or voice box is located.

The vocal folds can be manipulated by opening or closing them to produce sound. They may be narrowed for voiceless sounds such an "s" sound. At times they may touch lightly together so that they vibrate such as when we make a "zzzz" sound. When they are closed completely it is a glottal stop and no air passes through the larynx.

When the vocal folds vibrate they create the particular pitch of speech. Shift in pitch is related to the length, thickness, and degree of tension when the folds vibrate. The number of vibrations per unit of time and the intensity with which the bands are moved apart creates vocal tone.

Above the larynx is the pharynx. Sound waves arrive here to begin the process of resonation of the voice. In this cavity we take the vibrational sounds from the larynx and manipulate the walls of the cavity through shape and tension.

Located just above the larynx and behind the mouth, the pharynx also serves a pathway for breath and speech into the mouth or upward into the nasal cavities. The uvula, which is located at the back of the mouth and at the top of pharynx, acts as a directional aid in determining whether sound travels forward into the oral cavity (mouth) or upwards into the nasal cavity.

Here in the pharynx the quality of the sound of voice begins to be produced. Added tension in this passageway alters the quality of the sound. And with the passage of the sound from here to the oral or nasal cavity there is the determination of what types of sounds will ultimately be created.

Once the breath and sound is directed into either the nasal or oral cavity articulation occurs. In the English language certain sounds are directed upward into the nasal cavity for articulation. These sounds are the "n" and "ng" sounds.

Other articulation of sound occurs in the oral cavity. According to Wells:

> For General American English, the center or focus of oral resonance is generally mid-mouth.
> For many people, focusing resonance a bit more forward of mid-mouth actually helps to promote greater lip activity, which can result in clearer, crisp sounds. Bring it too far forward in the mouth, you will sound more British than American. If the center of resonance focus is too far in the rear of the mouth, you will sound guttural or even garbled (23–24).

Within the oral cavity are the articulators, which are the lower jaw, lips, teeth, gums, tongue, hard palate, and soft palate. The varying of these structures creates the sounds of language.

Importance of Breath Control

Controlling the breath is an essential element for good vocal control. Without control of the breath the speaking voice may sound winded or weak and proper vocal variety may not be achieved. When one is in control of the breath they may exert a greater control of the flexibility of vocal production and create greater vocal effect in their speaking.

Since the voice may be controlled by the breath, supporting the breathing apparatus and aligning it for greater use is of the utmost importance. Speaking may be said to start with a thought and that thought is then converted into speech, which is a physical activity. Only when breathing is controlled can that speech reach a freedom of expression desirable for communication.

A free deep intake of air pulled from the diaphragm will support the voice for speech. If one is breathing shallowly by simply expanding the lungs, the breath will remain unsupported and the speaker will not have the capacity to express longer units of thought.

Diaphragmatic breathing will also help the speaker strengthen the voice so as not to speak too much from the throat. Throat speaking will create a hoarse and weak vocal production that will quickly tire the voice.

When we breathe without thinking it is our diaphragm that is doing the work of inhalation and exhalation. Relaxing into this natural rhythm is the desired first step in understanding the use of the breathe for the purposes of speaking.

To check for diaphragmatic breathing, stand and place your hand on your upper abdomen just below the rib cage. Slowly draw in a breath. As you do so, you should notice that your abdomen should expand outward from your body. You will see your hand move in that same direction. Slowly push your hand against your abdomen while exhaling the air.

If you are not witnessing the natural inhalation and exhalation from the diaphragm you might try lying on the floor with a book on your stomach. As you lay there relax and breathe. Soon you should see the book rising and falling along with the rhythm of the inhalation and exhalation of air from the diaphragm.

Breathing Exercises

To get your body ready for good diaphragmatic breathing, do the following:

Stand up straight and tall with your legs shoulder width apart.

Stretch upwards with your arms reaching toward the ceiling.

Come up on your toes and balance.

Slowly drop back down to your heels.

Drop your fingers.

Drop your wrists.

Drop your elbows.

Drop your shoulders.

Drop your neck.

Drop your chest.

Roll down from the waist.

Hang for a moment from the waist feeling the small of your back fill with air.

Slowly roll the back upward. As you do this concentrate on stacking one vertebra on top the other. Take your time doing this until you slowly roll your neck upward and your standing up straight and tall.

As you reach the end of this you will be aligned properly for breathing and speech.

Now, let's relax the body a bit so that you aren't too rigid.

Drop your head forward and slowly roll your neck around in a circle. Do this three or four times one direction and then reverse direction.

Roll your shoulders back from your body in a circular motion lifting them up, pulling them back, and then circling back around. Do this circling three or four times and then reverse direction.

Shake your arms freely to loosen then up.

Standing up straight and tall, feet should width apart, breath in expanding the diaphragm.

Open your mouth by dropping your jaw and make a gentle "ahhhhh" sound as you exhale. Do this three times.

Next time concentrate on pulling in as much air as you can from the diaphragm and hold it. When you exhale this time relax your jaw and make a loud long "ahhhhhhh" sound letting the voice trail off as the last of the air is expelled from your lungs.

Finally stand and breathe normally in and out feeling the breath as it is supported by the diaphragm and is moving freely through an aligned body.

Breath Control Exercises to Eliminate Shallow Breathing

We sometimes forget that our breath control comes from our diaphragm, not our lungs. You don't want your collar bones or shoulders to raise and lower as you breathe, which indicates that you are breathing too shallowly. Try the following exercises to eliminate shallow breathing:

1. Place both hands on your upper chest with your thumbs facing your collar bones. Take a deep breath in and count from one to ten on your exhale. If you can feel any upward movement of your shoulders, use the pressure of your hands to prevent it.

2. Sit comfortably erect in an armless chair. Grab the bottom of the chair seat firmly with each hand. This should keep your shoulders from rising as you inhale and exhale feeling your diaphragm expand like a bellows on the inhale, and conversely contract on the exhale, noticing that your shoulders remain motionless.

3. While standing or sitting, count to four silently as you inhale, and count to four again silently as you exhale. Continue that count for several cycles of breathing, then increase the silent count to six on your inhale, and six on your exhale for several cycles of breath. Keep increasing your counts up to fifteen or more and you will develop great breath control. If you do this while walking any distance you can synchronize your steps to your counts, and get two kinds of exercise in!

3

"My singing voice is somewhere between a drunken apology and a plumbing problem."
—COLIN FIRTH

The Why and How of Recording Your Voice for Self-Assessment and Improvement

©wavebreakmedia/Shutterstock.com

Most people upon hearing their voice recorded have the same reaction, "That's not what I sound like!" But it is. It is the way the rest of the world hears you. Because when you speak, you hear your own voice both externally and internally; you are the only one who hears your voice in the manner that you do. On the one hand, you hear your voice through the sound waves that everyone else does as it arrives to your ear but on the other hand, you are also hearing it as it resonates within your own vocal instrument and therefore you hear something that no one else does.

Because as a speaker, you are interested in working on the quality of your voice as others hear it you need to objectively hear it while you are not speaking. The best way to do this is to record the voice. Using simple voice recording instruments that are probably already built into your computer, you can record a passage of text to be played back for a listen.

When listening for a first time, you probably will not like the sound of your own voice. Few people do because it doesn't sound the way they think it does. You may think that the recording instrument is faulty somehow but you will need to listen objectively and accept that, that is indeed the sound of your voice coming from the recording.

Once you get over the initial shock of hearing your voice as others hear it, you can start to analyze the sound of your voice for its strengths and weaknesses. After listening a few times to your recording, fill out the sheet for vocal analysis in this text indicating your strengths, weaknesses, and qualities.

By identifying your strengths, you can build on them in your vocal work. By identifying your weaknesses you can actively work to strengthen those areas of your voice that may need improvement.

This is simply step one in listening to your recording. Because you are still probably not as objective as you might be you can now let another class member or a friend listen to your recording and have them fill out the vocal analysis sheet for your voice. Comparing what you hear to what another person is hearing can be instructive and move you toward a more objective process of listening to your voice.

As you listen to your vocal recording, you can determine its quality.

Exercise for Listening to Your First Recording

While listening to your recording, have the following list handy to identify the quality of your voice.

adenoidal adjective
if someone's voice is adenoidal, some of the sound seems to come through their nose

appealing adjective
an appealing look, voice, and so forth. shows that you want help, approval, or agreement

breathy adjective
with loud breathing noises

brittle adjective
if you speak in a brittle voice, you sound as if you are about to cry

croaky adjective
if someone's voice sounds croaky, they speak in a low rough voice that sounds like they have a sore throat

dead adjective
if someone's eyes are dead, or if their voice is dead, they feel or show no emotion

disembodied adjective
a disembodied voice comes from someone who you cannot see

flat adjective
spoken in a voice that does not go up and down. This word is often used for describing the speech of people from a particular region.

fruity adjective
a fruity voice or laugh is deep and strong in a pleasant way

grating adjective
a grating voice, laugh, or sound is unpleasant and annoying

gravelly adjective
a gravelly voice sounds low and rough

gruff adjective
a gruff voice has a rough low sound

guttural adjective
a guttural sound is deep and made at the back of your throat

high-pitched adjective
a high-pitched voice or sound is very high

hoarse adjective
someone who is hoarse or has a hoarse voice speaks in a low rough voice, usually because their throat is sore

honeyed adjective
honeyed words or a honeyed voice sound very nice but you cannot trust the person who is speaking

husky adjective
a husky voice is deep and sounds hoarse (=as if you have a sore throat), often in an attractive way

low adjective
a low voice or sound is quiet and difficult to hear

low adjective
used for describing a deep voice or a sound that has a long wavelength

low adverb
in a deep voice, or with a deep sound

matter-of-fact adjective
used about someone's behavior or voice

modulated adjective
a modulated voice is controlled and pleasant to listen to

monotonous adjective
a monotonous sound or voice is boring and unpleasant because it does not change in loudness or become higher or lower

nasal adjective
someone with a nasal voice sounds as if they are speaking through their nose
End of DIV entry

orotund adjective
an orotund voice is loud and clear

penetrating adjective
a penetrating voice or sound is so high or loud that it makes you slightly uncomfortable

quietly adverb
in a quiet voice

raucous adjective
a raucous voice or noise is loud and sounds rough

ringing adjective
a ringing sound or voice is very loud and clear

rough adjective
a rough voice is not soft and is unpleasant to listen to

shrill adjective
a shrill noise or voice is very loud, high, and unpleasant

silvery adjective
a silvery voice or sound is clear, light, and pleasant

singsong adjective
if you speak in a singsong voice, your voice rises and falls in a musical way

small adjective
a small voice or sound is quiet

smoky adjective
a smoky voice or smoky eyes are sexually attractive in a slightly mysterious way

soft-spoken adjective
speaking or said in a quiet gentle voice

sotto voce adjective
in a very quiet voice

stentorian adjective
a stentorian voice sounds very loud and severe

strangled adjective
a strangled sound is one that someone stops before they finish making it

strangulated adjective
strangled

strident adjective
a strident voice or sound is loud and unpleasant

taut adjective
used about something such as a voice or expression that shows someone is nervous or angry

thick adjective
if your voice is thick with an emotion, it sounds less clear than usual because of the emotion

thickly adverb
with a low voice that comes mostly from your throat

thin adjective
a thin voice or sound is high and unpleasant to listen to

throaty adjective
a throaty sound is low and seems to come from deep in your throat

tight adjective
a tight voice or expression shows that you are nervous or annoyed

toneless adjective
a toneless voice does not express any emotion

tremulous adjective
if something such as your voice or smile is tremulous, it is not steady, for example because you are afraid or excited

wheezy adjective
a wheezy noise sounds as if it is made by someone who has difficulty breathing

wobbly adjective
if your voice is wobbly, it goes up and down, usually because you are frightened, not confident, or are going to cry

List compiled by http://www.macmillandictionary.com/us/thesaurus-category/american/words-used-to-describe-someone-s-voice

Exercise for Listening to Your Recorded Voice

1. Write down which adjectives from the previous list describe the sound of your voice.

2. Ask someone else to listen to your recording and have them list the adjectives that they believe describe your voice.

3. List what you like about your voice and what you might want to improve in your vocal quality and delivery:

Marking Your Text

Once you have a basic handle on the sound of your voice you are ready to start building on your strengths and working on your weaknesses. As we move toward isolating each of the elements of voice, you may want to use a system of marking your text to help you remember what you would like to do with your voice as you present. There is no one way of marking a text that is standard practice for all but the following markings found adapted from Alburger are a good place to start.

Underline (_____) emphasizes a word, phrase, or descriptive adjective.

Circle (O) key elements of conflict in the text.

Highlight or different color underline—resolution or nonresolution of conflict.

Arrow pointing UP—take the inflection on a word up

Arrow pointing DOWN—take the inflection on a word down.

Wavy line (~~~) modulates your voice or inflection.

Slash (/)—a short pause.

Double Slash (//) a longer pause.

Double Facing Arrows (←->) Extend duration of a sound.

Sample of a marked text

Gettysburg Address, Abraham Lincoln

> Fourscore/ and seven years ago our fathers <u>brought forth</u>, upon this conti-nent,/ a new nation, <u>conceived</u> in liberty and <u>dedicated</u> to the proposition that "all men are created equal."//
>   Now we are <u>engaged</u> in a great civil war, testing whether that nation, /or any nation so conceived and so dedicated,/ can long endure. We are <u>met</u> on a great battlefield of that war. /We have come to dedicate a portion of it, as a final resting place for those who <u>died</u> here, /that the nation might <u>live.</u> // This we may, in all propriety do. /But in a larger sense, <u>we cannot</u> dedicate, /<u>we cannot</u> consecrate, /<u>we cannot</u> hallow, this ground. //The brave men,/ living and dead, /who <u>struggled</u> here, have hallowed it, far above our <u>poor power</u> to add or detract. The world will little note/, nor long remember what we say here; /while it can never forget what they did here.//
>   It is rather for <u>us</u> the living,/ <u>we</u> here be dedicated to the great task remaining before us—that from these <u>honored dead</u> we take increased devotion to that cause for which they here gave the last <u>full measure</u> of devotion—that <u>we</u> here highly resolve that these dead shall not have died in vain, /that this nation shall have a <u>new birth of freedom</u>, /and that government <u>of the people</u>, /<u>by the people</u>, /for the people shall not perish from the earth.

ABRAHAM LINCOLN

These markings are only suggestive of what one might use to make nota-tions on a text. What is important is that as you discover through rehearsal what you want to do with a text to communicate a particular meaning, you want to be able to replicate that discovery. By using a notational system, either the one above or one of your own making, you can recapture the discovery of your rehearsal process.

Many professionals who use their voice to make a living will mark their scripts for vocal variety. Broadcasters routinely do this. Voice over actors may also engage in this process. In the heyday of radio drama, actors would often mark their texts. One of the most famous radio performances of all time was by Agnes Moorehead in the radio drama <u>Sorry, Wrong Number</u>. Moorehead repeated this performance more than once on the radio program <u>Suspense</u> and later in staged readings. If you visit Moorehead's archives, you will find the script that she used for each of those performances and the markings she used to remember what she wanted to do vocally with the text. In short, she was able to "set" the performance and recreate it by using her notational system.

Volume

©pathdoc/Shutterstock.com

Normal speech patterns only have slight differences in loudness, between 4 and 5 Hz (sound wave cycles per second), but screams can modulate very fast, varying between 30 and 150 Hz.

—LUC ARNAL

The primary responsibility that you have as a speaker is being easily heard by your audience. The audience should not have to strain to hear you. In order to fill the space with your voice, do not simply raise your voice to be heard but rather project your voice toward the furthest reaches of the audience. This notion of projection should help you to be able to carry even a whisper to the person sitting in the back row.

Projection is the ability to place the voice in the ear of every audience member with ease. It starts with supporting the voice from the diaphragm and directing the sound outward to fill the space. If we think of the voice as having physical properties, and we might, given that it starts deep in your body as an intake of air that is forced through the various internal speech making mechanisms, then we can think of your words issuing forth as sound waves that can be focused and projected throughout a space.

Think of your voice as something that you are throwing out into the world. Standing in front of an audience, you could look at the back wall of the space and think about throwing your voice hard enough to the wall that it might bounce back to you thus ensuring that all within the space will easily hear voice.

This focusing of the projection of the voice is the first element of volume that a speaker needs to attend to in order to be successful in delivering a message. One exercise that might be useful is to have students practice projecting the voice to one another.

Projection exercise

1. Have the students in the class pair up for this exercise and have them face one another in close proximity to each other (no more than a foot apart) in the center of the room.
2. One student in the pair will make a "pa" sound designed to project that sound to the other student but no further. Make sure that the student making the "pa" sound is supporting the sound with their diaphragm and is, in fact, pushing the "pa" sound from there and not from the throat. Have the students place their hand on their diaphragm to aid them in this process.

3. Once the first student has sent their "pa" sound their partner have the partner send a "pa" sound back.

4. Allow the students to send those sounds back and forth for a bit.

5. Once they are comfortable projecting from a distance of about a foot apart, have them each move a few steps further away from each other and repeat the exercise.

6. Each time the pair is comfortable at each distance sending the "pa" sound back and forth have them increase their distance.

7. Once students are at their farthest remove from one another sending the sound back and forth, instruct them to slowly walk toward one another making the "pa" sound back and forth.

This exercise in projection will help the student project the sound from their diaphragm in a focused way and allow them the experience of filling space from near to far. This will also start to attend to the physical nature of the sound of the voice.

Volume as an element of voice is not just concerned with getting the audience to hear you but is also used to create varying emotional and psychological effects in the minds of the audience. Raising and lowering the voice is also an aspect of **emphasis** wherein a greater weight is placed on certain sounds, words, or phrases by raising or lowering the volume of the voice. Within the English language, one needs to use the proper emphasis on certain syllables to create proper pronunciation. The word **syllable** for instance needs to have what is called a syllabic stress where the volume is greater on the first syllable of the word syllable—**syl**-la ble (Wells 77). The stress may also be on the last syllable or a middle syllable as well: see a-**bout** and con-**clu**-sive.

Volume also determines, in part, the attitude and tone of speech. According to Alburger, "The dynamic range of a performance is directly related to attitude and tone—from soft and intimate to loud and aggressive. Dynamic range is expressed as variations in the *volume* (loudness) of your voice as you speak" (75). This dynamic range communicates to the audience the attitude of the speaker. Is the speaker angry, calm, sad, anxious, or frustrated? The volume level will shift to appropriately communicate those emotions to the audience.

You may raise or lower the level of volume to give greater prominence to a word or phrase in order to match the emotional dynamic of the passage being spoken. Try these sample sentences and decide where the emphasis on raising or lower the volume will help communicate a particular sense of emotional meaning:

Exercise: Practice Sentences for Volume and Emphasis

Underline the words you wish to give emphasis to in each of the following sentences and then practice saying them aloud.

God heals, and the doctor takes the fees. Benjamin Franklin

Whenever a doctor cannot do good, he must be kept from doing harm. Hippocrates

I rather like the world. The flesh is pleasing and Devil does not trouble me. Elbert Hubbard

To become the spectator of one's own life is to escape the suffering of life. Oscar Wilde

Practical politics consists in ignoring the facts. Henry Adams

The sad duty of politics is to establish justice in a sinful world. Reinhold Niebuhr

It is well that war is so terrible—we would grow too fond of it. Robert E. Lee

In peace, sons bury their fathers; in war, fathers bury their sons. Herodotus

Fear ringed by doubt is my eternal moon. Malcolm Lowry

Anxiety is the interest paid on trouble before it is due. Dean William R. Inge

Profitability is the sovereign criterion of the enterprise. Peter Drucker

You build on cost and you borrow on value. Paul Reichmann

Education is indoctrination, if you're white—subjugation if you're black. James Baldwin

A child educated only at school is an uneducated child. George Santayana

The dignity of man lies in his ability to face reality in all its meaningless-ness. Martin Esslin

Man makes holy what he believes, as he makes beautiful what he loves. Ernest Renan

Life is a long preparation for something that never happens. William Butler Yeats

Life can only be understood backwards; but it must be lived forwards. Soren Kierkegaard

A truth that's told with bad intent—beats all the lies you can invent. William Blake

One way to define vocal emphasis is to think of it as strategically choosing which word(s) in a sentence to vocally "punch" with your voice so that they stand out to the ears of the listener. By separating out and playing with just that quality of your voice in the next few exercises you should see how your strategic choice of vocal emphasis influences the interpretation of the meaning of your message to your audience.

- When sixteenth US President Abraham Lincoln delivered the last lines of the Gettysburg Address to his audience of about 15,000 people at the dedication of the Gettysburg memorial soldiers cemetery on November 19, 1863, eyewitnesses report that he said it with the following emphasis (go ahead and read it out loud to hear how it sounds):

"that <u>this</u> nation, under <u>God</u>, shall have a <u>new birth of freedom</u>—and that government of the <u>people</u>, by the <u>people</u>, for the <u>people</u>, shall not perish from the earth." When spoken with the vocal emphasis on the repetition of "people," this elegant and timeless definition of the essence of democracy focuses the listener's attention on the enactors of government, the people. We often hear vocal reciters of the Gettysburg Address speak that passage with the following alternative choice of emphasis (again, say it out loud so you can hear the difference): . . .

"and that government <u>of</u> the people, <u>by</u> the people, <u>for</u> the people, shall not perish from the earth." Notice with the emphasis on "of," "by," and "for" rather than people, the listener's attention is focused on the structure of government, the acted upon rather than the actors. Government becomes the important subject of the idea, rather than the people/citizens who direct the course of government. A single difference in vocal emphasis can make all the difference in interpretation of meaning.

Let's take on all the possible shades of interpretive meaning a listener could make from being asked the following simple tongue twister:

- "Does your shirt shop stock socks with spots?"
  Say each of the following iterations out loud putting your vocal emphasis on the underlined word, and see how different the implied question becomes to the shop owner hearing it;
- "<u>Does</u> your shirt shop stock socks with spots?" Owner hears "Well, does it or doesn't it?"
- "Does <u>your</u> shirt shop stock socks with spots?" Owner hears "As opposed to the shirt shop across the street?"

- "Does your <u>shirt</u> shop stock socks with spots?" Owner hears "Your shirt shop, not your suspenders shop"
- "Does your shirt shop stock <u>socks</u> with spots?" Owner hears "Not slippers with spots, socks with spots"
- "Does your shirt shop stock socks with <u>spots</u>?" Owner hears "Not socks with stripes, socks with spots"
- Drawing from the following passages of famous American speeches, let's continue to appreciate the different effect that changing your choice of vocal emphasis can have on influencing audiences' attention to and consequent interpretation of the significant point of a message.
- Speak out loud each different choice of emphasis in the three iterations of the same passage from Senator Margaret Chase Smith's maiden speech to congress entitled "Declaration of Conscience" on June 1, 1950, in which she courageously took on Senator Joseph McCarthy's nefarious communist witch hunt against innocent citizens;
    a. "<u>I</u> speak as a Republican. <u>I</u> speak as a woman. <u>I</u> speak as a United States Senator. <u>I</u> speak as an American."
    b. "I <u>speak</u> as a Republican. I <u>speak</u> as a woman. I <u>speak</u> as a United States Senator. I <u>speak</u> as an American."
    c. "I speak as a <u>Republican</u>. I speak as a <u>woman</u>. I speak as a <u>United States Senator</u>. I speak as an <u>American</u>."
- Speak out loud the alternative emphasis choices in the two iterations from a passage from Dr. Martin Luther King's iconic "I Have a Dream" speech delivered on August 28, 1963 on the steps of Lincoln Memorial in Washington DC to hundreds of thousands of supporters of National Voting Rights Legislation:

"With <u>this</u> faith, we will be able to <u>work</u> together, to <u>pray</u> together, to <u>struggle</u> together, to <u>go to jail</u> together, to <u>stand up for freedom</u> together, knowing that we will be free one day."

"<u>With</u> this faith, we will be able to work <u>together</u>, to pray <u>together</u>, to struggle <u>together,</u> to go to jail <u>together,</u> to stand up for freedom <u>together</u>, knowing that we will be free one day."

- On June 6, 1984, forty-second US President Ronald Reagan delivered an address commemorating the fortieth anniversary of D-Day, when US troops stormed the Beaches of Normandy France to repel the Nazi German forces and turn the tide of World War II. He was speaking to the soldier survivors of that bloody battle, in tribute to their courage and sacrifice as he spoke the following last lines of the speech against the cliffs of Pointe Du Hoc in France. Decide, which set of emphasis choices you think are more powerful as you speak these stirring words out loud;

"<u>Strengthened</u> by their courage and <u>heartened</u>

by their valor and <u>borne</u> by their memory,

let us <u>continue</u> to stand for the <u>ideals</u> for which they <u>lived</u> and <u>died</u>."

"Strengthened by <u>their</u> courage and heartened

by <u>their</u> valor and borne by <u>their</u> memory,

let <u>us</u> continue to <u>stand</u> for the ideals for which

<u>they</u> lived and <u>died</u>."

Rate

> The trouble with talking too fast is you may say something you haven't thought of yet.
>
> —ANN LANDERS

Rate is simply the speed at which a person speaks. Conversationally, we may naturally speak rapidly (over 150 words per minute), but an overall slower rate is often preferred for any presentational speaking situation. In conversation, we need to exhibit a give and take relationship with those being spoken to. The conversation partner can stop a speaker who is going too fast to ask them to repeat what has been said. In presentational speaking, audiences are generally more passive and cannot stop the speaker as they present their speech. Taking time and care to produce a general rate of speech that is easy to digest for an audience becomes a baseline for using rate well.

The other end of the spectrum in difficult comprehension for audience members when it comes to rate is when the speaker speaks too slowly. Although with this slower rate the material may be easily digested, the audience may grow impatient and lose interest. It becomes too ponderous and audiences may have to piece together what was spoken, as they may have not received the full phrasing of the meaning of the text. They are left piecing the meaning back together.

Rate is controlled by **pauses**. We use pauses as an intentional means to control rate and the division of thought within speech. Curry, an elocutionist/expressionist practitioner in the late nineteenth and early twentieth century, taught that one must think the thought before producing the speech. Pauses are what come between the thoughts, whether they are short or long pauses that join one thought to the next showing the progression of an argument, a story, or an instruction. As we pause we slow down the rate with which we speak.

As one pauses they have an opportunity to think the next thought so that a new direction may be expressed, an extension of the previous idea continued, or to let a previous thought sink in before moving forward.

The other element associated with rate that must be discussed is **duration**. Duration is the amount of time spent on a particular sound. Sometimes we draw out vowels or consonants to emphasize their importance or to add color to their meaning. "I can't stand meatloaf," is a fairly simple sentence but with the use of duration, a speaker can emphasize how much they hate meatloaf by elongating the vowel sound in the word "stand." "I can't staaaaand meatloaf," helps determine the level of dislike. This is a matter of using duration of the vowel sound to show the meaning of your speech drawing attention to a state of mind.

Subordination

In some sentences with a number of clauses, some of the clauses are more important than others. In fact, some clauses read much as a parenthetical phrase that could be dropped without losing the overall meaning of the sentence. When encountering such a phrase, it is customary to use a slower rate for the main clauses and to speed up through the subordinate clauses. Thus the speaker is drawing attention to the greater meaning of the text and not emphasizing that which is not the heart of the message.

Exercises for diagnosing your habitual overall rate

The average speaking rate for the US English speaking speech community is generally acknowledged to fall in the range of between 125 and 150 words per minute. There are two ways to easily diagnose your own habitual overall speaking rate. You can count out a 125 to 150 word passage from a text, start a 60 seconds timer, then read the passage out loud naturally. When the 60 seconds runs out and the timer alarm goes off, you will know whether you read faster or slower than you'd like or were right where you want to be. The alternative is to read out loud your text for however long it is, note the starting time, note the ending time, count the words in the text, and divide by the number of minutes you read.

Exercise/Practice Sentences for Rate and Pause

Place a / where you wish to make a short pause and a // where you wish to make a longer pause.

If you can look into the seeds of time and say, which grain will grow, and which will not, speak then to me. Shakespeare

The future comes one day at a time. Dean Acheson

The difference between genius and stupidity is that genius has its limits. Anon

Doing easily what others find is difficult is talent; doing what is impossible for talent is genius. Henri Frederic Amiel

A loving person lives in a loving world. A hostile person lives in a hostile world: everyone you meet is your mirror. Ken Keyes, Jr.

It is well to remember that the entire population of the universe, with one trifling exception, is composed of others. John Andrew Holmes

What we can do for another is the test of powers; what we can suffer is the test of love. Brook Foss Westcott

The entire sum of existence is the magic of being needed by just one person. Vi Putnam

Make money and the whole world will conspire to call you a gentleman. Mark Twain

When you have told anyone you have left him a legacy, the only decent thing to do is to die at once. Samuel Butler

He that will not apply new remedies must expect new evils, for time is the greatest innovator. Francis Bacon

Every gain made by individuals or society is almost instantly taken for granted. Aldous Huxley

At is based on order. The world is full of 'sloppy Bohemians' and their work betrays them. Eduard Weston

An artist has been defined as neurotic who continually cures himself with his art. Lee Simonson

Cynicism is that blackguard of defect of vision which compels us to see the world as it is, instead of as it should be. Ambrose Bierce

We can destroy ourselves by cynicism and disillusion just as effectively as by bombs. Kenneth Clark

Pitch

©Stokkete/Shutterstock.com

Pitch is the raising or lowering of the tone or sound of the voice. It is described as high or low and the range in between. A **habitual pitch** is the pitch that we tend to speak in our normal conversational behavior. This pitch may or may not match what is described as **optimal pitch.** This pitch is that which is best for your own vocal mechanism when it is relaxed and open for projection. The habitual pitch is what one comes to through socialization and imitation from sources in the environment. Consequently, gender may play a role in habitual pitch. We tend to think that women should have a higher pitch than men and men a lower pitch than women. Sometimes, because of this gendering of the voice the habitual pitch for a woman or a man may be far from the optimal pitch for that person.

Finding the habitual and optimal pitch for a speaker is easy.

Exercise for finding habitual pitch

1. Students should stand and start to breathe in and out in a way that is natural for them.
2. Next, students should take in a breath and hold.
3. On the exhalation of the breath the student makes an "ahhh" sound.

4. This should be done a few times.

5. By the end of the exercise students can hear the pitch that they normal initiate speech.

Exercise for finding optimal pitch

1. Students should stand and start to breathe in and out deeply from the diaphragm.

2. Next, students should take in a breath and hold.

3. On the exhalation of the breath, the student relaxes the jaw and makes an "ahhhh" sound pushing from the diaphragm to project the voice forward.

4. This should be done a few times.

5. By the end of the exercise, the students can hear the pitch that is optimal for their own vocal mechanism.

After doing the two exercises, students will know how far away their habitual pitch is from their optimal pitch. When speaking to an audience, you should speak more from the optimal pitch, as you will be more relaxed and able to project effectively.

Pitch and Inflection

Your vocal **pitch** refers to how your voice would place on a musical scale if each single syllable you spoke was a note on that scale. Your **pitch range** refers to how many "notes" your voice can produce from its lowest to highest note. The average North American vocal pitch range is approximately sixteen notes or two octaves. Gifted singers have a twenty-four-note or three-octave range. Many of us have a more restricted pitch range. Let's stop here and get a ballpark estimate of your own pitch range by completing the following exercise:

Informal pitch range diagnostic: sit or stand erect so that your diaphragm is not pinched or restricted, take a deep breath in and "sing" up the scale in single note increments (la, la, la, la, la, la, la, . . .) starting at the lowest note you can hit without hurting yourself and singing single notes up to the highest note you can hit without straining your throat, counting each note (on your fingers is fine) as you go up to your highest note. Do not worry if you lack a perfect pitch or you hate singing, just give it a shot. When we do this together in class, it usually takes three attempts before everyone gets a semiaccurate and reliable count on their own pitch range. When we do it as a group, I describe the sound we make as just like the old Dolby sound system ad you would hear in theatres before the movie starts. We all begin and end on different notes but the sound as we each ascend together is really cool! So, how many notes did you count? I guarantee it was more than one, right? No matter how many notes we each have available, varying our pitch across syllables, words, and sentences is our goal. Your vocal **inflection** refers to your pitch pattern across words and sentences. Again, imagine that we place each syllable or word you speak as a note on a sheet of music. The more variety of low to high notes that you can see across the words and sentences you have spoken, the better your inflection variety.

Pitch and inflection exercises

In the North American English speaking speech community, there are a few generally accepted norms of listeners' interpretation regarding inflection patterns. One of them is that we tend to expect questions to end with a raised pitch inflection on the last word of the question. We are socialized to interpret that raised intonation as a question when we hear it.

- Try saying the following sentences out loud and see if they don't naturally inflect up on the last word. "Would you like to join me for lunch?" "Do you think it will rain today?"
- Another inflection norm is that we tend to expect most assertions, or claims to end with a lowered pitch on the last word. We are socialized to hear that lowered intonation as a statement of fact or assertion. Read the previous two sentences that begin with "Another inflection pattern . . . " out loud and see if you naturally lower your pitch on the last word of each sentence.

Your inability to utilize and strategically vary your full available range of low to high "notes" when you speak are the most direct causes of the dreaded audience coma-inducing monotone speaking voice, in which you speak every syllable and every word of every sentence on the same note. In general, this is much more likely to happen if you choose a manuscript mode of delivery as your memory aid, rather than the extemporaneous mode or impromptu mode. Most of us will be perceived by our listeners to have an effective and natural pitch variety in our regular, spontaneous conversations. Unfortunately, when given words to read from a paper or teleprompter, many of us lose that natural and unaffected pitch variety. A contributing factor could be that you lacked systematic training and practice reading out loud so you neither developed the craft nor the comfort using the manuscript mode of delivery. That is what this text is designed to help you with.

As mentioned earlier, **Inflection** is the shift of pitch upward or downward and is what creates the musicality of the voice and vocal variety in speech. Shifts in inflection give a musicality to the voice and help a speaker avoid a monotone delivery that will not guide the audience toward an understanding of a text. Some utterances have natural inflection shifts that help a speaker communicate such things as when a question is being asked, excitement is being expressed, or sadness is being indicated.

According to Wells, Rising or Upward Inflection is used to stress a syllable or word that is the most important in a sentence, to ask a yes or no question, to connect incomplete ideas such as lists, with dependent clauses, and to suggest uncertainty. Falling or downward inflection is used to make positive statements, to ask questions with interrogatives—who, what, when, where, and why, to finish lists and ideas, and to give an impression of uncertainty (55).

The use of inflection will help to clarify the meaning of the speaker's utterance. Because the English language uses shifts in pitch, which may be referred to as **intonation**, the audience is able to understand not just the sound of the word but why the speaker might by speaking that particular word. Proper place of stress on the syllable that leads to correct pronunciation is step one in using pitch changes and pitch changes on the most important word(s) of a message along with changes at the end of a message allows the audience to follow the emotional and psychological meaning of the text for the speaker.

It is in pitch variety that we hear the musicality of any given language. An individual speaker's use of pitch changes helps the listener determine the meaning of the utterance and also the emotional meaning behind the utterance.

Circumflex inflection is the process of shifting the pitch from up to down or down to up or up to down to up or down to up to down. So, in order to show surprise one might take the word "Oh" and use a circumflex inflection. In doing so, there would be a rise in pitch in the middle of voices the "Oh" sound and then a lowering of it back to the original pitch.

Rhetorical question intonation exercises

For speakers who are selling an idea, a mood, an action, a candidate, or a product, one of the most potent persuasive rhetorical style tools is the use of the rhetorical question. It is typically defined as a self-answering question, asked by the persuader to evoke a strategic preplanned psychological and/or verbal response from the audience, usually eliciting either a "yes" or a "no." The power of the rhetorical question is that by using the audience to provide the conclusion of a deductive or inductive argument, it strengthens the audience's commitment to your proposition or appeal and appears to come from them, not you. This puts them in control of the choice rather than feeling manipulated into a decision or choice.

Remember our earlier discussion of how listeners in the United States "standard" English speech community expect the inflection or pitch to go up on the last word of a question to pick up on the request. Sometimes this is true and you will want to make sure you are elevating the pitch note discernably on the last word in the question higher than the previous word. But sometimes to make sense of the question as it is constructed you should pitch the last word of the question on the same note as the previous word, and sometimes it makes sense to lower the note on the last word of the rhetorical question, even though that makes it sound like a claim. The important point is to make an intentional choice that maximizes the odds of evoking the audience response you want. Here are some examples of different choices on inflection at the end of rhetorical questions:

- In this powerful excerpt from Patrick Henry's famous 1775 exhortation of "Liberty or Death," he uses a series of rhetorical questions to get his audience to agree that the colonists have tried every possible reasonable argument with King George to no avail, thus the only alternative is to foment an armed revolution for independence. As you read the passage out loud, note that the first question requires that you inflect the last word "stronger" so that "strong" is higher than "er," but after that the pitch should go up a discernable note on each last word of every consequent question in order to cue the audience response of "no" to each question, and thus commit them emotionally and intellectually to the act of declaring war;

They tell us, sir, that we are weak; unable to cope with so formidable an adversary. But when shall we be stronger? Will it be the next week, or the next year? Will it be when we are totally disarmed, and when a British guard shall be stationed in every house? Shall we gather strength by irresolution and inaction? Shall we acquire the means of effectual resistance by lying supinely on our backs and hugging the delusive phantom of hope, until our enemies shall have bound us hand and foot?

- On August 19, 1992, Mary Fisher stood before the Republican Presidential Nominating Convention in Houston Texas and delivered a courageous rebuke to the party for remaining silent about the AIDS pandemic in a powerful personal appeal for compassion and action in her speech entitled "A Whisper of AIDS." Her rhetorical question to the relatively hostile audience needed to evoke a "yes" response, hence the need to make sure the note goes up on that most important last word of the question as you read the following out loud;

"We may take refuge in our stereotypes, but we cannot hide there long, because HIV asks only one thing of those it attacks. Are you human? And this is the right question. Are you human?

- We see the same kind of question asked for the same effect by Susan B. Anthony in 1873 as she spoke before people at 29 post offices all over Ontario, New York in hopes they might be on the jury that would hear her defend her arrest for voting illegally in the 1872 election:

"Webster, Worcester and Bouvier all define a citizen to be a person in the United States, entitled to vote and hold office.

The only question left to be settled now is: Are women persons?"

- Our last set of practice rhetorical questions comes from the Great American orator, statesman, and abolitionist activist, Frederick Douglass, in his July 5, 1852 address "What to The Slave is The Fourth of July" As you read this passage out loud, note that it is a good example of how not all last words should necessarily go up in a rhetorical question to effectively evoke the intentional meaning. When you get to the last question, pay attention to how it sounds to inflect the last word of the last clause on a discernably higher note or a discernably lower note, as if it were a claim though it be phrased as a question. Which version makes more sense to you?

Would you have me argue that man is entitled to liberty? That he is the rightful owner of his own body? You have already declared it. Must I argue the wrongfulness of slavery? Is that a question for Republicans? Is it to be settled by the rules of logic and argumentation, as a matter beset with great difficulty, involving a doubtful application of the principle of justice, hard to be understood? How should I look to-day, in the presence of Americans, dividing, and subdividing a discourse, to show that men have a natural right to freedom?

Note to the reader: All of the preceding manuscript excerpts were taken from http://americanrhetoric.com.

Exercises to stop the roller-coaster or sing-song effect

We have been discussing the importance of avoiding a monotonous vocal delivery pattern by maximizing pitch and inflection variety. Let us take a closer look at how to avoid falling into a too-consistent pitch pattern across all your sentences in the message, which creates a sing-song or rollercoaster effect. This occurs when you begin each sentence on a low pitch note, then go up discernably on each word to the middle of the sentence and then lower your pitch down a note on each word until you get to the last word. Notation-wise, it looks like a rollercoaster if we traced the consistent low–high–low pattern of notes in each sentence. Audience members stop discerning the words in the message and just "hear" the sound of your voice droning on and on as a background effect for their own drifting thoughts.

You should be able to clearly discern if you are falling into a too consistent or monotonous inflection pattern as you listen to an audio recording of you reading your message out loud.

The key to working on increasing your inflection variety across your text is to practice trying out each of the options of pitching your voice up a notch, on the same note, or down a notch on the last word or syllable of the last word in each sentence. Make notations indicating whether you are pitching the last word or syllable in each sentence up from the pre-vious word or syllable, on the same note as the previous word or syllable, or down from the previous word or syllable. Record yourself reading with each inflection choice to decide which choices retain the message impact you are aiming for, then note them down so you can hit them consistently in performance. Try practicing this strategy with one of the sample texts in the appendix. Practicing with a colleague, friend, or coach would be even more helpful to help you discern the difference between your pitch choices for each sentence ending. By making a strategic and meaningful choice that varies the pattern and honors the emotional and intellectual impact of each idea you are conveying, you maximize the fidelity and authenticity of your vocal delivery as well the active engagement of your audience.

Exercise/Practice Sentences for Pitch

Draw and arrow up or down where you might want to make a pitch change.

Life is an irreversible process and for that reason its future can never be a repetition of the past. Walter Lippman

I believe the future is only the past again, entered though another gate. Arthur Wing Pinero

Be thou as chaste as ice, as pure as now, thou shalt not escape calumny. William Shakespeare

He that flings dirt at another dirtieth himself most. Thomas Fuller

Bigamy is having one husband too many. Monogamy is the same. Erica Jong

A wise woman will always let her husband have her way. Richard Brinsley Sheridan

A man is never so weak as when a woman is telling him how strong he is. Anon

When women go wrong, men go right after them. Mae West

Cowardice, as distinguished from panic, is almost simply a lack of ability to suspend the functioning of the imagination. Ernest Hemingway

There is nothing wrong with making mistakes. Just don't respond with encores. Anon

Exercise for pitch change

1. Have the students pair off for this exercise.
2. Students should stand facing each other a few feet apart.
3. Student one will say the work, "Please."
4. Student two will respond by saying, "No."
5. The students will repeat their one word conversation a number of times trying to shift their pitch and intonation each time.
6. In doing the exercise the students will notice that not only will they want to shift their pitch but might also want to shift their volume or rate and that is fine however, they should focus primarily on how they shift pitch.

Pause

The most precious things in speech are the pauses.

—Sir Ralph Richardson

Although Pause has already been mentioned as an element that controls rate, a separate discussion of pause is needed to stress the importance of this form of nonvocalized emphasis. Pause is silence and silence around the utterance of our words helps control how those words are received by the audience; both in terms of meaning and in terms of emphasis.

A pause is first and foremost a way of separating out units of thought. Units of thought might be a sentence, a phrase, or a clause. In written communication, we see those units of thoughts as they are indicated by punctuation such as a period, a comma, a semicolon, an exclamation point, and so forth. But in order to indicate that same unit of thought in spoken communication the pause must be used to group the units of thought. When we read we give longer or shorter pauses to the types of punctuation. Shorter pauses are given to commas, colons, and semicolons which all appear in the body of a sentence. Conversely, longer pauses are given to those punctuations at the end of sentences such as periods, question marks, and exclamation points. There is no exact correlation to the amount of time given in spoken language to each of these punctuations except with the overall presentation of speech. So, when a speaker is speaking, there would be a clear indication that they pause for a shorter amount of time with the embedded within the sentence punctuation than they would with the end of the sentence punctuation.

Another way in which written communication uses the pause is in the paragraph endings, chapter endings, and other breaks within a text. These breaks signify that a new larger unit of thought is coming and in spoken language will require a longer pause than anything with or at the end of a sentence. As we have been taught in writing classes, we start a new paragraph to indicate a new thought and in spoken language a longer pause may help indicate that a new thought is coming.

Pauses are also a chance for a speaker to let a thought sink in for an audience. When speakers move too quickly from unit of thought to unit of thought the audience may lose some of what is being communicated. Pause, long or short, may give an audience a chance to process the information before moving forward. This of course is related to the overall rate being used by the speaker.

Finally, pauses are used as a moment for the speaker to think into the upcoming thought. In this moment of silence, the speaker is processing where they have been and where they want to move next. As such, the speaker will be ready to express the meaning of the next unit of thought as an extension of the previous thought or a shift in idea or mood. This moment allows the speaker to prepare for other shifts that might need to follow such as shifts in pitch and inflection, rate, or volume.

Often times, speakers, especially novice speakers, are afraid of silence and hence of pauses. They erroneously believe that if they are not speaking at all times they are failing to communicate with their audience, that the audience might think they have forgotten what they need to say next, or that silence in not meaningful. Nothing could be further from the truth. Silence and pausing are a necessary and meaningful part of speech. The control of rate, helps in the shifting of thought, and allows for the digestion of previous speech by the audience, and is one of the speaker's most powerful and under-utilized tools for getting and retaining your listener's attention, which is the first necessary requirement for any message.

Use the single slash and double slash markers to note when you want to use pauses. Practice with the sample texts in the appendix and record yourself. We are confident you will see the noticeable improvement in the vocal power you have given the verbal message by adding strategic pause to your repertoire.

Exercises to minimize vocal fillers (like, uhm, you know, whatever, OK?)

Since we are practicing the power of the pause, this is a good time to acknowledge that when we speak in any mode other than manuscript, we often need to search in our mind for the next "just right" word to convey our thoughts. Unfortunately, we tend to fill the time we are searching with a meaningless word place—filler, and we each have our favorite, whether it occurs at the beginning of the thought "uuhmmm . . . .," the middle "I was like," "you know," or at the end "whatever," "am I right?" "OK?"

Three to five "uhhmms" sprinkled throughout a three- to five-minute extemporaneous or impromptu oral message will probably not be noticed by listeners, and in fact can convey positive credibility for you the speaker because they signal to your audience that you are authentically present in the moment and thinking about your message rather than delivering something canned or rote. The problem is that when vocal fillers become noticeable in their frequency, they can ruin your credibility with your audience. Your listeners cannot possibly focus on the message because they are caught up in counting the dysfunctional disfluency markers that are flying out of your mouth without you even noticing.

So, what can you do? Despite their potential effectiveness, we do not recommend tasing yourself or taking a shot of alcohol everytime you say "uhhm," because of the obvious negative side effects of either method. We do know that in any good multi-step recovery program, your first task is to notice you have a problem. We become so habituated to vocal fillers that we literally do not hear ourselves using them. First you have to develop a signal that will get you to pay attention every time you say "uuhmm" (maybe a bell, a clicker, or a rubber band snap on your wrist). This is another situation where external coaching helps at the beginning. Having a friend, colleague, or coach give that signal, and starting the sentence over without the vocal filler is the first recommended step in the process of eliminating unwanted vocal fillers.

Here's where silence comes in. What you have to do is replace the habit of filling the silence with an "uuhmm" by just letting the silence be. Silence is a speaker's friend. Use it. Remember that in real time the pause you need to take to find the word you want to say is rarely discernable to your listener. In fact, it looks like you are being thoughtful, which makes you seem smarter or more concerned with your audiences' welfare, so again you build positive credibility points by just being silent until you find the word you are looking for. Practicing being silent rather than filling that tiny silence with a vocal filler is what we call the cold turkey approach. Sometimes we aren't ready to go cold turkey, and we need a patch to tide us over the rough time. If you can't handle the silence at the beginning of your utterance, go with a real word like "well" to replace "uhhmm." Since "well" is a real word, your listener might assume you are using it intentionally, so it doesn't have the negative distracting effect of "uhhmm."

If you practice consistently over a period of time, you really can eliminate your over-use of vocal fillers. The fluency you will gain will take you a long way on your journey to be an in-demand speaker, we promise.

Exercise Sentences for Practice

Use a / for a short pause and // for a longer pause in each of the following sentences

I'm not hard, I'm frightfully soft. But I will not be hounded. Margaret Thatcher

They are proud in humility; proud that they are not proud. Robert Burton

It has been said that though God cannot alter the past, historians can—it is perhaps because they can be useful to Him in this respect that He tolerates their existence. Samuel Butler

The rich experience of history teaches that up to now not a single class has voluntarily made way for another class. Joseph Stalin

For most singers the first half of the career involves extending one's repertoire, the sand half trimming it. Ethan Mordden

Life exists in the universe only because the carbon atom possesses certain exceptional properties. James Jeans

Science is built of facts the way a house is built of bricks; but an accumulation of facts is no more science than a pile of bricks is a house. Henri Poincare

Nothing links man to man like the frequent passage from hand to hand of a good book. Walter Sickert

Reading after a certain (time) diverts the mind too much from its creative pursuits. Any man who reads too much and uses his own brain too little falls into lazy habits of thinking. Albert Einstein

Articulation

Speak clearly, if you speak at all; carve every word before you let it fall.

—OLIVER WENDELL HOLMES

©lassedesignen/Shutterstock.com

Articulation is the process by which a speaker makes each syllable of a word clearly understandable to the audience. By clearly enunciating each syllable the speaker ensures that each word uttered is intelligible. Crisp and clear articulation is necessary to ensure that audiences understand what is being spoken. This is, perhaps, after adequate volume the most necessary base line for communicating spoken language.

When a speaker mumbles, overlaps speech or assimilation, and drops the end sounds of words the result is inarticulate speech. When a person mumbles, they are not working their speech instrument properly. They may have a mush mouth or lazy mouth and are not properly employing their jaws, lips, and tongue to crisply and decisively form the sounds of the words. When overlapping speech occurs, it is generally when a speaker fails to distinguish between two separate words. If the words "She's sad," are together in a sentence there may be an assimilation of the two words and it gets pronounced as "She'sad." This overlap of the two words fails to account for the distinct repetition of the "s" sound at the end of one word and the "s" sound at the beginning of the subsequent word. When speakers fail to pronounce the last sound of a word, they are defaulting to what might be fine in conversational speech but is considered sloppy in formal speaking. Not pronouncing the end "g" in words may be the most common error. Saying, "goin" instead of "going" is an example.

Clear articulation is one of the signs of an educated speaker. So long as the speaker does not overarticulate (exaggerating sounds so they sound unnatural), the articulate speaker has a greater chance of being understood and impressing an audience. To illustrate, I was once part of a team interviewing a potential candidate for a position as a professor of Speech Communication. It was troubling, to say the least, that this candidate kept dropping the "g" sound when talking about Public Speaking. So, every time he spoke of "Public Speakin'" his chances of securing the position dropped as well.

One particularly good way to practice clear articulation is to practice speaking tongue twisters. Tongue twisters are a sequence of words that may be difficult to pronounce because of alliteration (repetition of consonant sounds) or a slight variation of a consonant sound. Particularly, if a speaker tries to say a tongue twister quickly they may find themselves mangling the sentence or phrase.

Try the following tongue twisters

For each of the following speak the tongue twister at a normal rate and then try increasing the rate of speech until you are speaking it clearly at top speed.

Toy boat, toy boat, toy boat.

Black bugs blood, black bugs blood, black bugs blood.

Topeka bodega, Topeka bodega, Topeka bodega.

Irish wristwatch, Irish wristwatch, Irish wristwatch.

Red Buick Blue Buick, Red Buick Blue Buick, Red Buick Blue Buick.

Once you have mastered those try the following

I slit a sheet, a sheet I slit, and on that slitted sheet I sit.

Or this: One smart fellow; he felt smart. Two smart fellows; they both felt smart. Three smart fellows; they all felt smart. And they all felt smart together!

When working on articulation, it is important to note that there may be a sense of artificiality in the work. You might, understandably, say that by so clearly articulating you are not really speaking the way people actually speak. This is true in so far as that is not the way people speak conversationally. There are certainly situations that a speaker may find himself or herself in where they want to approximate a more conversational approach to their speech and their articulation. Knowing why you are doing this and having the ability to heighten articulation are ways in which we may be simply shifting our speech codes to adapt to various audiences. As Alburger notes,

> To achieve a conversational and believable delivery, it is often necessary to violate some of the basic rules of crisp articulation. However, it is important to understand and to master the correct way to do something before you can effectively do that thing incorrectly and make it believable. In other words, you've got to do good before you can do bad, believably (77).

Pronunciation

Knowing the correct, standard way to say or pronounce a word is an extremely important task for any speaker. When we mispronounce a word, the impression we leave upon an audience is a negative one. Checking the correct, and by correct we mean the standard agreed upon, pronunciation of words is a job that must be taken seriously. Faking your way through pronunciations may lead to embarrassment.

When the frail eighty-three-year-old General Douglas MacArthur returned to his beloved West Point Military Academy in 1962 to deliver his famous Farewell Speech to the cadets (Duty, Honor Country), his final words were "Today marks my final roll call with you, but I want you to know that when I cross the river my last conscious thoughts will be of The Corps, and The Corps, and The Corps. I bid you farewell" If you don't know that the letters p and s in the word "corps" are supposed to be silent, and you read that passage pronouncing the word as "corpse," you can see what we mean by invoking the perils of not being 100% sure that you have mastered the correct pronunciation of every word that comes out of your mouth.

Pronunciation is a matter of understanding the proper way to utter a word based on the way in which various groups understand and agree the way in which a word should be spoken. Different groups may have a different way of pronouncing a particular word. Speaking the word correctly for the speech community in which it is uttered is the guiding principle for good pronunciation.

Words can be broken down into the individual syllables for pronunciation. The combination of syllables or phones is a phoneme. By focusing on the sound of each phoneme in a word a pronunciation for the word is obtained. As you look for pronunciation of various words you are looking for how the word is pronounced within the speech community of which you are a member or of which you speaking. Being able to code switch those pronunciations when there is a difference may help the speaker communicate clearly for different audiences.

If you think you know the correct pronunciation, but aren't sure you should consult a dictionary. For speakers, it would be even better to use the online dictionaries that will have an audio link to click on that will say the word for you. Listening to this pronunciation a few times and repeating it will get the appropriate pronunciation in your mind.

When speakers use an incorrect pronunciation of a word, chances are that there is someone in the audience who does know the correct pronunciation. When that moment of miss-pronunciation occurs, the audience member with knowledge of the correct pronunciation will judge the speaker negatively and the speaker's credibility will be weakened.

So, checking well in advance on any words you might be uncertain of in terms of pronunciation is always a good idea. Then you will be able to get the right pronunciation, practice it, and eliminate any wrong pronunciations from your memory.

Earlier the International Phonetic Alphabet (IPA) was mentioned as something that this book would not be using in any detail to aid in vocal improvement. However, pronunciation is one area in which the IPA could be very useful to the speaker. Learning the various symbols for consonant and vowel sounds in the IPA is way to transcribe those difficult to pronounce words on the page so that you can keep those sounds in your mind. This link to the IPA and its uses will help you use this method: http://www.internationalphoneticalphabet.org.

Phrasing

Phrasing is the ability to set a group of related words together to express a unit of thought. Those units of thought are separated by a pause. Phrasing creates a particular flow of delivery, a rhythm, and variations of tempo, which affect the overall tone of delivery. Emphasis and duration may also be used to create phrasing in the absence or in conjunction with pauses.

When seeking to create meaning in spoken communication, you must use phrasing to create an interpretation that will guide the audience toward a specific meaning that is intended by the speaker. By phrasing the units of thought or using emphasis and duration to create a flow of speech, the speaker makes a choice of how they intend a text or utterance to be understood.

This passage from Gerard Manley Hopkins' poem "God's Grandeur," can be used to illustrate how one can create subtle interpretive meanings in a text.

And all is seared with trade; bleared, smeared with toil;

This passage may be broken up by pausing at the punctuation points that are in the line of the poem. And most would do this. However, there are other options. Try reading aloud each of the following pausing at the / sign and hear the difference of the rhythm of the phrasing and the slight variation of meaning that occurs.

And all/is seared with trade; bleared, smeared with toil;
And all/is seared with trade; bleared, smeared/with toil;
And all is seared with trade; bleared, smeared/with toil;

Now working with emphasis, putting a louder or softer volume on the word or changing the pitch level, speak the line with the word in bold with emphasis.

And **all** is seared with trade; bleared, smeared with toil;
And all is **seared** with trade; bleared, smeared with toil;
And all is seared with **trade**; bleared, smeared with toil;

Again, notice the subtle shifts in meaning and rhythm given the line with each of these readings.

If one uses duration of vowels sounds, again, meaning and rhythm of the phrasing will shift. Try speaking the following by elongating the vowel sounds in the words in bold print.

And **all** is seared with trade; bleared, smeared with toil;
And all is **seared** with trade; bleared, smeared with toil;
And all is seared with trade; **bleared, smeared**, with toil;

When working with a printed text, one may want to try several ways of phrasing to uncover various interpretations of the text. Through repeated speaking of the text in a variety of ways, the speaker will come to a comfortable phrasing that makes the most sense to the speaker.

Tone/Attitude

We often refuse to accept an idea merely because the tone of voice in which it has been expressed is unsympathetic to us.

—Friedrich Nietzsche

When a speaker speaks, you can discern the way they would like their audience to respond by noting their tone of voice or their attitude about what they are saying. The attitude of the speaker helps guide the audience toward the response that the speaker desires them to have. A monotone voice that lacks any variation of pitch, rate, or volume will not accomplish a clear tone or attitude that will allow the audience to determine how they should respond to what is being spoken.

If, for instance, a speaker were to say, "You are really smart" in a sincere tone of voice the receiver of the statement would understand that the speaker means to encourage the listener. However, if the speaker to were to say the same sentence in a sarcastic manner the listener would determine that the speaker does not mean to call them smart at all but perhaps is really meaning the opposite. As the speaker changes the attitude of the sentence they will manipulate the various elements of voice: volume, rate, pitch, pause, and phrasing to approximate the desired tone/attitude.

Attitudinal tone of voice is the combining of all the other elements of speech together to create meaning in speech. This process is achieved when the speaker is thinking thoughts rather than mere words. Thinking the thought before speaking will help the speaker arrive at an appropriate attitude before speaking.

The following is a partial list of some attitudes that a speaker might speak:

Tone/attitude words

1. Accusatory—charging of wrong doing
2. apathetic—indifferent due to lack of energy or concern
3. awe—solemn wonder
4. bitter—exhibiting strong animosity as a result of pain or grief
5. cynical—questions the basic sincerity and goodness of people

6. condescension; condescending—a feeling of superiority
7. callous—unfeeling, insensitive to feelings of others
8. contemplative—studying, thinking, reflecting on an issue
9. critical—finding fault
10. choleric—hot-tempered, easily angered
11. contemptuous—showing or feeling that something is worthless or lacks respect
12. caustic—intense use of sarcasm; stinging, biting
13. conventional—lacking spontaneity, originality, and individuality
14. disdainful—scornful
15. didactic—author attempts to educate or instruct the reader
16. derisive—ridiculing, mocking
17. earnest—intense, a sincere state of mind
18. erudite—learned, polished, scholarly
19. fanciful—using the imagination
20. forthright—directly frank without hesitation
21. gloomy—darkness, sadness, rejection
22. haughty—proud and vain to the point of arrogance
23. indignant—marked by anger aroused by injustice
24. intimate—very familiar
25. judgmental—authoritative and often having critical opinions
26. jovial—happy
27. lyrical—expressing a poet's inner feelings; emotional; full of images; song-like
28. matter-of-fact—accepting of conditions; not fanciful or emotional
29. mocking—treating with contempt or ridicule
30. morose—gloomy, sullen, surly, despondent
31. malicious—purposely hurtful
32. objective—an unbiased view—able to leave personal judgments aside
33. optimistic—hopeful, cheerful
34. obsequious—polite and obedient to gain something

35. patronizing—air of condescension
36. pessimistic—seeing the worst side of things; no hope
37. quizzical—odd, eccentric, amusing
38. ribald—offensive in speech or gesture
39. reverent—treating a subject with honor and respect
40. ridiculing—slightly contemptuous banter; making fun of
41. reflective—illustrating innermost thoughts and emotions
42. sarcastic—sneering, caustic
43. sardonic—scornfully and bitterly sarcastic
44. satiric—ridiculing to show to make a point, teach
45. sincere—without deceit or pretense; genuine
46. solemn—deeply earnest, tending toward sad reflection
47. sanguineous—optimistic, cheerful
48. whimsical—odd, strange, fantastic; fun

Taken from http://www.mshogue.com/AP/tone.htm

Courtesy of Dawn Hogue

These tones and/or attitudes may correlate to particular emotions both positive and negative. Following is a list of possible positive and then possible negative emotions.

Positive Emotions	Negative Emotions
Happy	Sad
Joyful	Angry
Loving	Mad
Liking	Grumpy
Lusting	Tearful
Sweet	Devastated
Pride	Horrified
Appreciative	Disgruntled
Hope	Hurt
Faith	Annoyed
Thrilled	Aggravated
Overcome	Hating
Overjoyed	Despise
Respectful	Depressed
Supportive	Sick
Serene	Fear
	Guilt
	Jealousy
	Anxiety
	Frustration
	Envy
	Shame

Exercise for Attitude/Tone

Record one of the following sentences using two different attitudes. As you listen back to the recording note how you shifted the various elements of speech to create the different tone/attitude.

Anarchy is against the law. Graffiti

We are never so happy no so unhappy as we imagine. La Rochefoucauld

No one has ever loved anyone the way everyone wants to be loved. Mignon McLaughlin

Love is a kind of military service. Latin Proverb

An atheist is a man who has no invisible means of support. Fulton Sheen

There is a crack in everything God has made. Ralph Waldo Emerson

The cleverest woman finds a need for foolish admirers. Anon.

A woman without a man is like a fish without a bicycle. Gloria Steinam

The devil's name is dullness. Robert E. Lee

The secret of boring people lies in telling them everything. Voltaire

After recording list, hear what you did in each reading to manipulate the various qualities of voice.

4

Podcasting

©Kzenon/Shutterstock.com

Podcasting is the process of sharing your knowledge, experience, or desires online on a webpage. Anyone who has an expertise or a desire to reach a particular audience through the Internet may want to consider doing podcasting. In addition to starting your own podcasting page, there are opportunities for voice-over work to be done on the webpages of other's who are in business or want a variety of voices for their own pages.

Podcasting is made easier these days by the advance of technology and easy to use recording devices oftentimes loaded on to personal computers and laptops. The MacBook, for instance, comes loaded with Garage Band, which is set up for podcasting. There are also free downloads such as Audacity that can be loaded on to a computer for quick podcasting purposes. More professional set-ups can be purchased to set up a home studio.

Most Home Audio Workstations are easy to use and a little time spent exploring the system in use will result in allowing you the ability to podcast and start loading on to your own page or sending off to a client for their use.

On a program such as Garage Band or any other program loaded on to a laptop, the microphone is built in to the device and will pick up clearly. For better quality, though, an external microphone might be needed and a pop screen attached to filter out impurities in the recording.

It is important to find a quiet place to record so that the recording does not pick up ambient sounds from the environment. Even the humming of a central air system might get picked up during recording and may need to be turned off for the duration of the recording session.

When recording you should have your texts laid out for easy perusal. Rustling of pages is an unwanted noise that could be picked up by the recording equipment. So, laying the pages out side by side or on a music stand will aid in moving from page to page.

Before recording, you should be in a comfortable position that will allow you to express yourself completely. If sitting, you should sit up straight in order to breathe effectively from the diaphragm. Standing while recording will ensure better posture and will allow the speaker use of their whole body to express themselves while speaking.

If video is involved then stage management of appearance and environment will be involved. Dressing appropriately to the podcast, in this case, will be necessary. Monitoring of gestures and facial expression will also become important. In addition, the setting of the recording will need to look professional.

When recording for your own purposes you will have written your own text and will know instinctively the attitude or tone of the piece. You will use your vocal qualities such as changes in volume, pitch, and rate in order to communicate that attitude. However, if you are recording for a client you will need to know precisely what the client wants in terms of sound for the podcast. When recording for the client do not be afraid to ask exactly what is expected from the recording so that you can deliver it.

When recording in a relaxed and comfortable position you should remember to speak as if your voice is reaching that one person listening to the podcast. There is an intimacy in viewing a podcast that calls for a conversational and yet dynamic delivery. Particularly if you are speaking from your own script, make sure to sound conversational and natural. A more extemporaneous sounding delivery is to be expected in this type of speaking.

If you are reading copy for a business for their podcast be cognizant of what they want you to achieve vocally. If they are selling product make sure you sound persuasive. If they are informing the public about their services, a clear explanatory tone is needed to communicate the material.

Podcasting is a wide-open area for vocal exploration. As technology continues to bring us closer together and the means for using the technology gets easier, it is a good idea to avail yourself of opportunities to get your ideas out there or to market your voice to others who need voice-over artists to speak on their websites.

Broadcasting

©Olena Yakobchuk/Shutterstock.com

Those who use their voices in the broadcasting arena work in journalism, as disc jockeys, public affairs programming, voice-over for commercials and narration for documentaries, and in special programming such as talk shows, informational programming, and children's shows. Across this wide array of work the voice is of paramount importance.

It should be noted that in broadcasting you might need to code switch to a more standard American accent to succeed. Much of broadcasting still prefers this particular sound of voice particularly for nationally broadcast shows. This is not to say that other accents cannot succeed, particularly in local markets. However, to move into a national market one may need to pay attention to the ability to code switch to a more standard American accent.

Two important factors can come into play in announcing for broadcasting: analyzing the structure and analyzing the mood of the text. By analyzing the structure of a text for broadcasting, one can see the subtle and not so subtle shifts that will need to occur in giving it voice. Once the shifts are noted, the talent can then determine what the mood for each of these structural shifts should be.

As Hyde says, "Radio and television announcers have one overriding purpose: *to effectively communicate ideas and feelings to others* (24). What one communicates to the audience is who they are not an imitation of someone else. Hyde stresses this when he writes: "True communication as an announcer begins when you learn *who you are, reflect yourself in your delivery, and realize that you are speaking to individuals, not to a crowd* (24). Media announcers are in the position of being listened to in the homes of the audience. As such, that audience wants to feel as if they are being spoken to directly. A sense of who the speaker is will help them receive the information being spoken. You then need to then convey the ideas and feelings associated with your text.

There are many types of performance situations that an announcer may find themselves in that require competence: "ad-libbing, ad-libbing from notes, impromptu speaking, script reading, script reading with preparation, and script reading from cold copy" (Hyde 24). Each of these skills takes practice to achieve the level of competence desired.

Students who want to get better at these skills should seek out practice texts such as those found on Edge Studio's website https://www.edgestudio.com/script-library.

By practicing with sample scripts you can analyze the structural elements of the text and then try to capture the mood or moods to convey the message.

Sermonic Speaking

©bikeriderlondon/Shutterstock.com

Preachers are most visible to the public on Sunday mornings when they are in the pulpit speaking to the congregation. This may be the only time that most members of the congregation see the preacher all week long. It is in this Sunday morning church service that the preacher brings the community together in shared faith and worship.

Preachers, ministers, and priests all need to attend to the quality of their vocal delivery to make the most of that hour or so of time that they have the undivided attention of the congregation. Since this may be their only contact throughout the week with many in their congregation, they need to make a strong impact not just by what they say but how they say it which includes how they use their vocal instrument to communicate.

There are, in most church services, two different types of text that are delivered by the preacher. The first is the sermon that is what many consider to be the centerpiece of the service. The second is the reading of scripture that is a communicating of the sacred word of the Bible.

The sermon in many mainstream Protestant Denominations is prepared by the minister or preacher him or herself. It is the text created by them that is to speak directly to that particular congregation. The message may be of urgent need by the congregation, a seasonal offering, or a way of teaching the doctrine of the church. As such the preacher will be creating a text that he or she knows will speak directly to their congregation.

In this capacity, the preacher is a public speaker and must attend to all the manner of speaking that is standard for good public speaking. When focusing on the voice, the preacher will be concerned with adequate volume and projection, changes in pitch, use of strategic pauses and emphasis, and a rate that is easy to follow.

The preacher must at all times be aware of the space in which she or he is speaking. They are bound by the social contract of the congregation to reach each person of the congregation. As such they must fill the physical space. Often times this is not so much a matter of projecting into the space but a matter of using the audio equipment effectively. Most churches these days have their preachers in front of a microphone or on a portable mic that is worn on their lapel or is worn on their head. You should check how much that mic picks up the voice, how close you must have your mouth to the mic for that to occur, and if a shift of the head to look around while speaking will continue to adequately pick up the voice.

A dynamic delivery that matches the subject matter of the sermon is necessary in order to keep the attention of the congregation. A flat or monotone delivery will put the congregation to sleep and they will be looking at their watches wondering how much longer this sermon will go on. Connecting with the congregation vocally is a vital job of the preacher.

So, he or she must be adequately heard and they must change pitch to avoid a monotone delivery. Thinking clearly about the message before speaking it will aid in this process. How does the preacher want the audience to feel and respond to what is said will help determine the pitch and the rate and the use of pause and the use of vocal emphasis. It is a process of thinking about first, what do you want to say? And then, how do I want the audience to feel as a result?

After thinking about the sermon itself the preacher ought to think about the presentation of the scripture. As many preachers are using a particular passage of scripture to base their sermon upon, the scripture itself will need to be read aloud.

Often times, the reading of the scripture is not given much attention. It seems to be just a warm-up to the sermon proper. However, it could be argued that the sermon is dependent on the scripture and therefore the scripture should be emphasized as an equal part of the presentation and given as much care in its vocalization.

The process of reading scripture aloud is part of the art of oral interpretation. Oral interpretation is a process of matching the voice in a text with that of the speaker in order to communicate that message to an audience. As such, the preacher will need to put him or herself in the place of the speaker or persona in the text and then try to match their vocal qualities.

There are many different genres of literature present in the Bible and each may need a different approach in presenting them. It makes a difference if one is speaking a passage of poetry or prose from the scripture. Understanding how each of those texts operates and what each of those voices embedded in those texts demand of a speaker is part of what a preacher needs to discern before giving it voice.

There are many texts devoted to helping in speaking the scripture aloud through the art of oral interpretation. If we go back in the history of the field of speech communication one such text was written by S. S. Curry titled *Vocal and Literary Interpretation of the Bible.* This early work set the stage for later works in the field. This text discusses the various types of literature found in the Bible and how to approach them vocally.

There are, of course, more contemporary texts to be found that cover much of the same material as Curry. An examination of that literature will help the preacher maximize their oral interpretive skills in speaking scripture.

The preacher has multiple vocal tasks in any church service. The two mentioned here, the sermon and the reading of scripture are just two of them. Other tasks include the speaking of prayer, the call to worship, and asking for an offering from the congregation.

In all of these vocal tasks, the preacher needs to be vocally alive and must modulate the voice to meet the task at hand. This will keep the flow of the service interesting for the congregation and allow for smooth transitions from one task to another.

As practice for speaking scripture, try the following passages to awaken the voice to the task at hand.

Bible verses

4 Love is patient, love is kind. It does not envy, it does not boast, it is not proud. **5** It does not dishonor others, it is not self-seeking, it is not easily angered, it keeps no record of wrongs. **6** Love does not delight in evil but rejoices with the truth. **7** It always protects, always trusts, always hopes, always perseveres. 1 Corinthians 13:4-7 New International Version

Note that in this passage of lyrical scripture there is a list. To capture the essence of each thing listed about love, the speaker may want to vary the vocal response to each thing mentioned. A shift in pitch, rate, volume, or phrasing will help each item stand out on its own as special.

In the following passages from Luke is the Parable of the Good Samaritan. Note that the story that is being told contains multiple voices and perspective from which to speak. The speaker of this text needs to indicate the shifts in voice from narrative to character voice throughout.

25 On one occasion an expert in the law stood up to test Jesus. "Teacher," he asked, "what must I do to inherit eternal life?"
26 "What is written in the Law?" he replied. "How do you read it?"
27 He answered, "'Love the Lord your God with all your heart and with all your soul and with all your strength and with all your mind'[a]; and, 'Love your neighbor as yourself.'[b]"
28 "You have answered correctly," Jesus replied. "Do this and you will live."
29 But he wanted to justify himself, so he asked Jesus, "And who is my neighbor?"
30 In reply Jesus said: "A man was going down from Jerusalem to Jericho, when he was attacked by robbers. They stripped him of his clothes, beat him and went away, leaving him half dead. **31** A priest happened to be going down the same road, and when he saw the man, he passed by on the other side. **32** So too, a Levite, when he came to the place and saw him, passed by on the other side. **33** But a Samaritan, as he traveled, came where the man was; and when he saw him, he took pity on him. **34** He went to him and bandaged his wounds, pouring on oil and wine. Then he put the man on his own donkey, brought him to an inn and took care of him. **35** The next day he took out two denarii[c] and gave them to the innkeeper. 'Look after him,' he said, 'and when I return, I will reimburse you for any extra expense you may have.'
36 "Which of these three do you think was a neighbor to the man who fell into the hands of robbers?"
37 The expert in the law replied, "The one who had mercy on him."

Jesus told him, "Go and do likewise."

Luke 10:25–37

Sample sermon excerpt

In the following sermon note that the minister is making an argument and as such the stress of that argument should be emphasized vocally through shifts in pitch and volume. Also there are quotes of both prose and poetry throughout that contain the voices of multiple speakers that need to be differentiated from the voice of the minister.

I Have Been To the Mountaintop

Dr. Scott Dillard

Let me start with the words of the Rev. Dr. Martin Luther King, Jr.

"Well, I don't know what will happen now. We've got some difficult days ahead. But it doesn't matter with me now. Because I've been to the mountaintop. And I don't mind. Like anybody, I would like to live a long life. Longevity has its place. But I'm not concerned about that now. I just want to do God's will. And He's allowed me to go up to the mountain. And I've looked over. And I've seen the promised land. I may not get there with you. But I want you to know tonight, that we, as a people, will get to the promised land. And I'm happy, tonight. I'm not worried about anything. I'm not fearing any man. Mine eyes have seen the glory of the coming of the Lord."

Courtesy of Dr. Scott Dillard

These words were spoken by Dr. King, April 3, 1968, to the striking sanitation workers in Memphis, Tennessee. He was, of course, assassinated the next day. Martin Luther King was, in my estimation, a prophet. We do well each year to pause and think of his legacy and of his prophecy. We do well to reflect on what he accomplished in this country for freedom and equality. We do well to honor the man and his legacy. King tells us that he has had a glimpse of the promised land, that it is with God that he has had such an experience, and that he is paving the way for us all to get to that promised land. King was obviously on a path to enlightenment and had gotten far enough along that he could see the goal. King, then, like so many prophets before him came back to share the vision and to give a hand up to those on the path behind him rather than going off alone into the promised land. He is like Buddha in that he stayed here to teach us. Even in his physical absence, his legacy still serves as a measure by which we might chart our own course. He is like Moses in that he has lead his people to the land that he, in his own lifetime may not occupy. He sacrifices himself so that others may learn from his journey and follow his path.

There are many paths to the mountaintop and King was on one of them. He was positioned to see the world from the vantage point of a particular time and place and it was under those conditions that he was to strive for a glimpse of the promised land. He walked a path that was blazed by many African American preachers who had come before him. He was on their path and yet he was also charting new territory. It is that way with us all. We all are on a path that we hope will take us to the mountaintop to glimpse paradise. We are all striving for that enlightened experience.

Each religious faith represents a path to the top of the mountain toward enlightenment, salvation, or eternal understanding and knowing. Each of those paths has been trod by generations of believers who have marked the territory. It is, at times, a comfortable journey, which can be full of reassurances that you are on the "right" path and that you will get your just reward upon arriving at the summit. Each of the paths has sureness about the validity of their way. Some, in fact, insist that there way is the only way. In the Christian Gospel of John, Jesus says, "I am the way and the truth and the life. No one comes to the Father except through me." (John 14:6 NIV) One commentator, A. W. Tozer, uses the passage to prove that no Christian believer should compromise their belief and offers this thought: "No one comes to the Father except through Jesus Christ. No one! No one! Because only Christ has paid the sin-debt for humankind. We cannot acknowledge as a way to the Father anything except the only way."

Similarly in Islam we have the sentiment expressed in this way, La ilaha ill Allah, Muhammad-ur rasul-ullah. There is no God but Allah and Muhammad is the Messenger of Allah. Indeed, in Islam Muhammad is thought to be the seal of the prophets. The seal of the prophets is accomplished upon the arrival of Muhammad. Other authentic prophets had appeared before Muhammad but in Muhammad, Islam reached its definitive form. There would be no valid prophets after Muhammad. So, this comes after Jesus, acknowledging his role as a prophet but not the last word at all.

Of course, the Jews reject both of these prophets and are still waiting for the messiah to come. In the messianic version of Judaism, and that is admittedly only one form of Judaism, when the Messiah appears all will acknowledge the one God of Judaism.

This reminds me of the words of Ramakrishna:

Mother, Mother, Mother! Everyone foolishly assumes that his clock alone tells correct time. Christians claim to possess exclusive truth…Countless varieties of Hindus insist that their sect, no matter how small and insignificant, expresses the ultimate position. Devout Muslims maintain that Koranic revelation supersedes all others. The entire world is being driven insane by this single phrase: "My religion alone is true." O Mother, you have shown me that no clock is entirely accurate. Only the transcendent sun of knowledge remains on time. Who can make a system from Divine Mystery? But if any sincere practitioner, within whatever culture or religion, prays, and meditates with great devotion and commitment to Truth alone, Your Grace will flood his mind and heart, O Mother. His particular sacred tradition will be opened and illuminated. He will reach the one goal of spiritual evolution. Mother, Mother, Mother! How I long to pray with sincere Christians in their churches and to bow and prostrate with devoted Muslims in their mosques! All religions are glorious.

Instructional Speaking

To teach is to create a space in which the community of truth
Is practiced...a rich and complex network of relationships
In which we must both speak and listen, make claims on others,
And make ourselves accountable. (XII)

PALMER, PARKER, J. (1993)

Reading "Green Eggs and Ham" out loud for the hundredth time and making it sound exciting. Delivering your favorite lecture on the early civil rights movement and wanting your students to feel as if they were experiencing it. Negotiating conflicts on the playground, or in the lunchroom. Comforting a distraught student in your office. Calming an angry parent in a phone conversation. Advocating for more funding for fieldtrips in front of the school board. Just an ordinary day in the life of a teacher, in which your voice must inspire, entertain, stimulate, captivate, convince, relax, and rally a variety of audiences every day you are on the job.

Research on teacher communication behavior and student learning outcomes has long confirmed the significance of teacher vocal qualities in influencing student perceptions of teacher clarity, credibility, and communication competence as well as student cognitive, and affective learning (Brophy, Coker, and Burgoon; Comadena, Hunt, and Simonds; Frymeier, Guerrero and Miller; Rosenshine and Furst; Rubin and Feezel). As Rubin confirms, "Impressions formed about teachers' communication competence are largely based on teachers' oral communication abilities." (254)

Developmentally grounded research on the kinds of communication concerns teachers express has also identified a vocal effectiveness component embedded in the many of the larger concern categories. Teacher communication concerns have been defined as "constructive frustration or anticipation of a future problem which involved participation in face to face interaction" (Staton-Spicer and Bassett 140). In a recent article examining emergent themes across ten years of graduate teaching assistants' communication concerns statements, Dannels uncovered ten emergent teacher communication concerns: exhibiting command of the material, balancing authority and rapport, dealing with communication anxiety, engaging students, managing perceptions, juggling roles, resolving grading complexities, being memorable, negotiating flexibility, and overcoming cultural differences (90). Sample teacher concerns statements that reflected balancing authority and rapport included "finding the appropriate voice in which to communicate with students….finding the balance between being too overbearing or not strict enough, too nice or too mean, rigid and inaccessible or easy to walk over" (Dannels 91). Concern statements about dealing with communication anxiety referred to stuttering and speaking really fast (Dannels 92). Concern statements about effectively engaging students included "crafting my lectures to students in a conversational tone," and "I might find the subject interesting, but how might I communicate that excitement to students?" (Dannels 93). Concerns about overcoming cultural differences centered on teachers' own accents being different for students and thus difficult to understand, and their own inability to understand student accents (Dannels 98).

It is clear that instructional communication research has confirmed the importance of vocal effectiveness in honing the art and craft of teaching excellence. We hope you are convinced that cultivating your strongest authentic voice as a teacher is a worthy endeavor.

In terms of methods for diagnosing and developing your vocal delivery strengths as a teacher, we recommend a combination of audio and/or videotaping along with using a consultant or colleague. As faculty development expert and consultant Seldon notes, "Watching a videotape replay can bring out important but forgotten details and bring teaching strengths and weaknesses into sharper focus. Some teachers are able to watch a videotape and recognize immediately how to improve their teaching. But most teachers need faculty colleagues or instructional improvement specialists to help analyze their teaching and to suggest modifications" (101). His words apply to analyzing your vocal strengths and weaknesses as well as higher inference teacher communication behaviors and you and your colleague or consultant can fruitfully use any of the observational or self-assessment forms included in our text for diagnosis and assessment. A second recommended resource for instructor communication assessment advice as well as forms is Cooper and Simonds.

Courtroom Speaking

©bikeriderlondon/Shutterstock.com

Lawyers rely upon their voice to make an argument in order to sway a judge or jury about the innocence or guilt of the accused. Whether they are the prosecutor or the defense lawyer, they are telling a story about how something happened. They are attempting to get agreement on the veracity of their story over the story of the opposing counsel.

Like all other speaking situations, courtroom speaking makes use of variety in vocal delivery in volume, rate, and pitch. A clear story needs to emerge that is compelling to judge and jury. Making use of all of the aspects of vocal delivery will help in creating such a story.

In speaking of pitch in the courtroom, Garner argues that a lower range of pitch will be more readily received than higher pitches which might come across as irritating (20). Learning to lower your pitch will help you avoid sounding like you are whining or that you sound childish.

Garner also states that one should speak with deliberation and force; not speaking too fast, too loudly, or too quietly.

> If you speak rapidly, your listeners will have trouble understanding what you've said. You also risk getting ahead of your own thoughts. If you speak hesitantly or softly, you may inadvertently signal that you're not confident about what you are saying (25).

When speaking of the pause, Garner rightly points out that silence does work for a speaker. He summarizes the use of the pause in this manner:

> It can give your audience a moment to consider
> what you just said; it can signal a transition
> from one point to the next; it can invite
> questions in response to the point you just
> made; or it can give you a change to gauge how
> the audience is reacting to your message (28).

Another area that Garner speaks to that is key for the courtroom speaker is pronunciation. One must know the proper preferred English pronunciations of words, legal terms, and proper names. It will reflect poorly on the speaker if they mispronounce any of these.

Putting together the elements of clear, articulate, forceful speaking patterns in the courtroom will help the lawyer make a favorable impression. It is not enough to have the facts on your side. Remembering that the arguing of a case is an act of persuasion and that the voice itself can aid in the act of persuasion is enough to make a speaker in a court of law want to develop their vocal skills to their greatest capacity.

Political Speaking

©a katz/Shutterstock.com

In our democratic society we are all potential political speakers. Whether we are actively running for office, speaking before our local city council, or speaking in front of a rally for a cause, we are all taking part in political speech. In each of these cases, a clear passionate voice is needed to get people to vote for you, sway your elected officials, or rally the troupes to a cause.

Much has been made of the manner in which politicians' deliver their speeches and the delivery of speeches may make or break them. When Howard Dean was running for President, he was roundly criticized after the Iowa primary for making a screaming sound that many in the media found unbecoming. It became a defining factor in his campaign and he quickly lost favor with the voters.

Tapping in to the tone of the voting public is key to the politician. She or he must match their audience in enthusiasm and desire. The tone of their speech, therefore, should parallel that of their audience's feelings.

But a good politician will often go a step further and try to inspire their audience to even greater heights. After tapping in to the audience's tone, they should take them somewhere new to show them the future. If an audience is angry with the establishment and the politician simply reflects that anger in their manner of speech, they leave them no solutions to the problem. The next step for the politician is to soften the tone to show the audience a new possible future where their anger can be channeled in to production solutions.

When speaking to a local government to try to sway them to take action that you deem desirable, one should approach with respect for the elected officials in order to get them to hear your arguments. They are more likely to hear your point of view on an issue if they feel that from your delivery of your message that you respect them and their position.

After showing in tone your respect for their work, you can argue your case passionately and articulately to get them on your side. They are more likely to be taken by an argument that meets them half way by deferring to their office but also firmly speaking your own point of view.

At a political rally, your main point is to rally the troups to action. Here you need to be all about passion. Your passion for the issue and your passion for a particular path forward need to be foregrounded. This is where an emotional outpouring that matches that of the audience is needed.

Remember that you are preaching to the choir at a rally and your main job is to keep them moving forward. You are there to inspire with your vocal delivery. So, a range of tone, shifts in pitch, rate, and volume will help you keep the audience interested and ready to continue in their fight.

In all political speaking, we are telling a story that we want heard. In our democratic society, we use our voices to convince our fellow citizens that what we believe they would benefit by believing too. So, a strong story is one that makes great use of all of the elements of voice.

5

Practice Texts

Sonnet XXIX

When, in disgrace with fortune and men's eyes,
I all alone beweep my outcast state
And trouble deaf heaven with my bootless cries
And look upon myself and curse my fate,
Wishing me like to one more rich in hope,
Featur'd like him, like him with friends possess'd,
Desiring this man's art and that man's scope,
With what I most enjoy contented least;
Yet in these thoughts myself almost despising,
Haply I think on thee, and then my state,
Like to the lark at break of day arising
From sullen earth, sings hymns at heaven's gate;
For thy sweet love remember'd such wealth brings
That then I scorn to change my state with kings.

—William Shakespeare

Jabberwocky

'Twas brillig, and the slithy toves
    Did gyre and gimble in the wabe:
All mimsy were the borogoves,
    And the mome raths outgrabe.

"Beware the Jabberwock, my son!
    The jaws that bite, the claws that catch!
Beware the Jubjub bird, and shun
    The frumious Bandersnatch!"

He took his vorpal sword in hand;
    Long time the manxome foe he sought—
So rested he by the Tumtum tree
    And stood awhile in thought.

And, as in uffish thought he stood,
  The Jabberwock, with eyes of flame,
Came whiffling through the tulgey wood,
  And burbled as it came!

One, two! One, two! And through and through
  The vorpal blade went snicker-snack!
He left it dead, and with its head
  He went galumphing back.

"And hast thou slain the Jabberwock?
  Come to my arms, my beamish boy!
O frabjous day! Callooh! Callay!"
  He chortled in his joy.

'Twas brillig, and the slithy toves
  Did gyre and gimble in the wabe:
All mimsy were the borogoves,
  And the mome raths outgrabe.

—Lewis Carroll

Nature, the gentlest mother

NATURE, the gentlest mother,
Impatient of no child,
The feeblest or the waywardest,—
Her admonition mild

In forest and the hill   5
By traveller is heard,
Restraining rampant squirrel
Or too impetuous bird.

How fair her conversation,
A summer afternoon,—   10
Her household, her assembly;
And when the sun goes down

Her voice among the aisles
Incites the timid prayer
Of the minutest cricket,   15
The most unworthy flower.

When all the children sleep
She turns as long away
As will suffice to light her lamps;
Then, bending from the sky,   *20*

With infinite affection
And infiniter care,
Her golden finger on her lip,
Wills silence everywhere.

The Tell-Tale Heart

TRUE!—nervous—very, very dreadfully nervous I had been and am; but why will you say that I am mad? The disease had sharpened my senses—not destroyed—not dulled them. Above all was the sense of hearing acute. I heard all things in the heaven and in the earth. I heard many things in hell. How, then, am I mad? Hearken! and observe how healthily—how calmly I can tell you the whole story.

It is impossible to say how first the idea entered my brain; but once conceived, it haunted me day and night. Object there was none. Passion there was none. I loved the old man. He had never wronged me. He had never given me insult. For his gold I had no desire. I think it was his eye! yes, it was this! He had the eye of a vulture—a pale blue eye, with a film over it. Whenever it fell upon me, my blood ran cold; and so by degrees—very gradually—I made up my mind to take the life of the old man, and thus rid myself of the eye forever.

Now this is the point. You fancy me mad. Madmen know nothing. But you should have seen me. You should have seen how wisely I proceeded—with what caution—with what foresight—with what dissimulation I went to work! I was never kinder to the old man than during the whole week before I killed him. And every night, about midnight, I turned the latch of his door and opened it—oh so gently! And then, when I had made an opening sufficient for my head, I put in a dark lantern, all closed, closed, that no light shone out, and then I thrust in my head. Oh, you would have laughed to see how cunningly I thrust it in! I moved it slowly—very, very slowly, so that I might not disturb the old man's sleep. It took me an hour to place my whole head within the opening so far that I could see him as he lay upon his bed. Ha! would a madman have been so wise as this, And then, when my head was well in the room, I undid the lantern cautiously-oh, so cautiously—cautiously (for the hinges creaked)—I undid it just so much that a single thin ray fell upon the vulture eye. And this I did for seven long nights—every night just at midnight—but I found the eye always closed; and so it was impossible to do the work; for it was not the old man who vexed me, but his Evil Eye. And every morning, when the day broke, I went boldly into the chamber, and spoke courageously to him, calling him by name in a hearty tone, and inquiring how he has passed the night. So you see he would have been a very profound old man, indeed, to suspect that every night, just at twelve, I looked in upon him while he slept.

—Edgar Allen Poe

The Monkey's Paw

IN the brightness of the wintry sun next morning as it streamed over the breakfast table Herbert laughed at his fears. There was an air of prosaic wholesomeness about the room which it had lacked on the previous night, and the dirty, shrivelled little paw was pitched on the sideboard with a carelessness which betokened no great belief in its virtues.

"I suppose all old soldiers are the same," said Mrs White. "The idea of our listening to such nonsense! How could wishes be granted in these days? And if they could, how could two hundred pounds hurt you, father?"

"Might drop on his head from the sky," said the frivolous Herbert.

"Morris said the things happened so naturally," said his father, "that you might if you so wished attribute it to coincidence."

"Well, don't break into the money before I come back," said Herbert, as he rose from the table. "I'm afraid it'll turn you into a mean, avaricious man, and we shall have to disown you."

His mother laughed, and following him to the door, watched him down the road, and returning to the breakfast table, was very happy at the expense of her husband's credulity. All of which did not prevent her from scurrying to the door at the postman's knock, nor prevent her from referring somewhat shortly to retired sergeant-majors of bibulous habits when she found that the post brought a tailor's bill.

"Herbert will have some more of his funny remarks, I expect, when he comes home," she said, as they sat at dinner.

"I dare say," said Mr. White, pouring himself out some beer; "but for all that, the thing moved in my hand; that I'll swear to."

"You thought it did," said the old lady soothingly.

"I say it did," replied the other. "There was no thought about it; I had just—What's the matter?"

His wife made no reply. She was watching the mysterious movements of a man outside, who, peering in an undecided fashion at the house, appeared to be trying to make up his mind to enter. In mental connection with the two hundred pounds, she noticed that the stranger was well dressed and wore a silk hat of glossy newness. Three times he paused at the gate, and then walked on again. The fourth time he stood with his hand upon it, and then with sudden resolution flung it open and walked up the path. Mrs. White at the same moment placed her hands behind her, and hurriedly unfastening the strings of her apron, put that useful article of apparel beneath the cushion of her chair.

She brought the stranger, who seemed ill at ease, into the room. He gazed at her furtively, and listened in a preoccupied fashion as the old lady apologized for the appearance of the room, and her husband's coat, a garment which he usually reserved for the garden. She then waited as patiently as her sex would permit, for him to broach his business, but he was at first strangely silent.

—W.W. JACOBS

Sample Evaluation Sheets

STUDENT NAME _____

Volume
Overall Effectiveness
_____Excellent
_____Satisfactory
_____Needs Improvement
Checklist for Volume
_____Easily heard throughout the space
_____Varied as to the material being presented

Rate
Overall Effectiveness
_____Excellent
_____Satisfactory
_____Needs Improvement
Checklist of Rate
_____Varied as to the material being presented
_____Pauses used appropriately

Pitch
Overall Effectiveness
_____Excellent
_____Satisfactory
_____Needs Improvement
Checklist for Pitch
_____Varied as to the material being presented
_____Clear emotions and feelings expressed
_____Clear expression of specific meanings

Articulation
Overall Effectiveness
_____Excellent
_____Satisfactory
_____Needs Improvement
Checklist for Articulation
_____Vowels and Consonants clearly differentiated
_____Crispness of sound

Speaker feedback form

SPEAKER NAME _____

Please provide your honest responses for the speaker by circling all that apply:

Effective vocal emphasis that conveyed the emotion and conviction of the message

Too monotone

too consistent on inflection

too soft overall, lost volume at end of sentences

excellent vocal emphasis choices varied effectively throughout

Effective rate of delivery

Too fast (over 150 words per minute all the way through)

Consistently between 125-150 wpm overall

Consistently between 125-150 wpm and varied effectively from fast-slow within the message

Use of dramatic pause to emphasize important words, phrases, or sentences

No discernable pauses before or after key phrases, sentences, or passages

Effective noticeable pauses for emphasis before or after key ideas and images

Crisp articulation of vowels and consonants and **correct pronunciation** of all words

Several words mispronounced

Noticeable dropping or distortion of vowels or consonants within words

Crisp articulation of vowels and consonants

No mispronunciations

How **well rehearsed and comfortable** with the manuscript did the speaker appear to be?

Appeared very under-rehearsed with 0-49% eye contact with all audience members

Appeared somewhat under-rehearsed with 51-75% eye contact with all audience members

Appeared adequately rehearsed with 75-100% eye contact with all audience members

How well did the speaker "lift the words off the page" and **make you forget they were reading to you**?

Overall never forgot they were

Forgot they were reading at moments

Completely forgot they were reading

Additional comments

I really appreciated that you:

It might be even more effective if:

Manuscript reading self-evaluation

_____

Please type your responses

1. Take me through what you did to prepare and practice for this presentation (what exactly did you do, when did you do it, and how did you do it). Looking back, what exactly would you do differently in terms of pre-speech preparation and practice?

What I did to prepare and practice before the presentation:

What I'd do differently to prepare and practice if I could do it again:

For each of the skills below, use your own experience, **quote your peer feedback in the relevant category (and provide the relevant peer rating average), and prove to me that you listened to your video** to thoroughly analyze the strengths and suggested improvements of each component of your reading. Use the back of the page or additional pages to complete each response.

Vocal and Physical Delivery:

75% eye contact with my audience

Couldn't see me slide the pages on the podium,

Overall stately rate at or below 150 words per minute (wpm),

Avoided too consistent of an inflection pattern,

Maximized pitch variety,

Effective vocal emphasis,

Strategic use of discernable pauses,

Volume loud enough overall and varied effectively,

Correct pronunciation, and crisp articulation,

Looked and sounded like I was well rehearsed and comfortable,

Gestured naturally,

Posture and body movement effective,

Hit the time limit.

Strengths
Peer feedback evidence:
Video evidence:

What I'd do differently and why
Peer feedback evidence:
Video evidence:

One thing you want to keep in your repertoire for the next presentation because you have evidence it is a skill you have already mastered:

One thing you want to make sure you do differently next time and how will you know (assess) that you've accomplished it?

My overall impression of how pleased I was with my voice after listening to it was (please circle one of the following)

1	2	3	4	5
Extremely displeased	Somewhat displeased	No feeling either way	Somewhat pleased	Extremely pleased

Works Cited

Alburger, James R. *The Art of Voice Acting,* 3rd ed. Boston: Focal Press, 2007. Print.

Brophy, J. "Teacher Influences of Student Achievement." *American Psychologist* 41 (1986): 1069–1077. Print.

Coker, D.A., and J.K. Burgoon. "The Nature of Conversational Involvement and Nonverbal Encoding Patterns." *Human Communication Research* 13 (1987): 463–494. Print.

Comadena, M.E., S.K. Hunt, and C.J. Simonds. "The Effects of Teacher Clarity, Nonverbal Immediacy, and Caring on Student Motivation, Affective, and Cognitive Learning." *Communication Research Reports* 24 (2007): 241–248. Print.

Cooper, Pamela J., and Cheri J. Simonds. *Communication for the Classroom Teacher*, 7th ed. Boston: Allyn & Bacon, 2003. Print.

Curry, S.S. "Importance of Studying the History of Elocution and Vocal Training." *Proceedings of the National Association of Elocutionists,* 1895 in Richard Haas and David A. Williams, The Study of Oral Interpretation: Theory and Comment, Indianapolis: Bobbs-Merrill, 1975.

Dannels, D. P. "Teacher Communication Concerns Revisited: Calling into Question the Gnawing Pull Towards Equilibrium." *Communication Education* 64 (2015): 83–106. Print.

Frymier, A.B. "A Model of Immediacy in the Classroom." *Communication Quarterly* 42 (1994): 133–144. Print.

Garner, Bryan A. *The Winning Oral Argument*. St.Paul: Thomson/West, 2009. Print.

Glenn, Ethel C., Phillip J. Glenn, and Sandra Foreman. *The Articulate Voice*, 4th ed. Boston: Allyn and Bacon, 1998. Print.

Guerrero, L.K., and T.A. Miller. "Associations between Nonverbal Behaviors and Initial Impressions of Instructor Competence and Course Content in Videotaped Distance Education Courses." *Communication Education* 47.1 (1998): 30–43. Print.

Herrick, James A. The *History and Theory of Rhetoric: An Introduction*, 3rd ed. Boston, MA; Allyn and Bacon, 2005. Print.

Hyde, Stuart. *Television and Radio Announcing*, 10th ed. Boston: Houghton Mifflin, 2004. Print.

Palmer, P.J. *To Know as We Are Known: Education as a Spiritual Journey*. New York; HarperCollins, 1993. Print.

Rodenburg, Patsy. *The Need for Words: Voice and the Text*. New York: Routledge, 1993. Print.

Rosenshine, B.V., and N.F. Furst. Research on Teacher Performance Criteria. *Research in teacher education*. By B.O. Smith. Englewood Cliffs, NJ: Prentice Hall, 1971. 27–72. Print.

Rubin, R., and J. Feezel. "Elements of Teacher Communication Competence." *Communication Education* 35 (1986): 254–268. Print.

Ryan, Halford. *Classical Communication for the Contemporary Communicator*. Mountain View, CA; Mayfield Publishing Company, 1992. Print.

Seldin, Peter, and Associates. *Changing Practices in Evaluating Teaching: A Practical Guide to Improved Faculty Performance*. Bolton, MA; Anker Publishing Co. 1999. Print.

Staton-Spicer, A.Q., and R.E. Bassett. "Communication Concerns of Preservice and Inservice Elementary School Teachers." *Human Communication Research* 5 (1979): 138–146.

Wells, Lynn K. *The Articulate Voice: An Introduction to Voice and Diction*, 4th ed. Boston: Pearson, 2004. Print.

Index

A

Articulation, 12, 13, 55–56
    tongue twisters, 56–59
Attitude, 61–64
Audacity, 67–68

B

Bible verses, 74–75
Breath control
    exercises to eliminate shallow
        breathing, 16
    importance of, 13–14
Breathing
    exercises, 14–15
    mechanics of, 11–13
Broadcasting, 69–70

C

Chatauqua movement, 5
Cicero, Marcus Tullius, 3–4
Circumflex inflection, 42–43
Code shifting, 9
Courtroom speaking, 80–81

D

Demosthenes, 3
Dialect of speech accent, 8–9
Diaphragmatic breathing, 14
Duration, 34

E

Elocutionary movement, 4–5
Emphasis, 27, 31–32
    practice sentences for, 29–30

G

Gorgias of Leontini, 3

H

Habitual pitch, 39
    exercise for finding, 39–40
Herrick, 2
Hippias of Elis, 3

I

Inflection
    defined, 41
    pitch and, 40–46
    shifts in, 42
Instructional speaking, 77–79
International Phonetic Alphabet (IPA),
    9–10, 59
Intonation, 42
IPA. *See* International Phonetic Alphabet

L

Legacy/value/history, of voice training for
    speakers, 2–7
Lyceum movement, 5